CW00701504

MOTIVESTIONS

MOTIVESTIONS
The Missing Key to Living Your Best Life

MICHAEL JENET

Guide Point North Publishing
COLORADO, USA

Guide Point North Publishing
An imprint of Journey Institute Press,
a division of 50 in 52 Journey, Inc.
journeyinstitutepress.org

Library of Congress Control Number: 2024932399
Names: Jenet, Michael
Title: MOTIVESTIONS
Description: Colorado: Guide Point North Publishing, 2024
Identifiers: ISBN 979-8-9894379-1-7 (hardcover)
Subjects: BISAC:
SELF HELP / Personal Growth / Happiness |
SELF HELP / Communication & Social Skills |
SELF HELP / Affirmations

First Edition
Printed in the United States of America

1 2 3 4 5 21 33 45 67 89

This book was typeset in Caslon Pro / Tyros Pro

Contents

For Dafna

Nothing would be possible or worth it without you.

Foreword
From the publisher

As the publisher of Journey Institute Press and all our imprints, I should also say that I am the author of this work. I originally wrote this book in 2014. It was published under the title *ASK: The Questions to Empower Your Life*.

That wasn't my idea. It was my publishers' at the time. He didn't like the title MOTIVESTIONS because he thought no one would know what it meant and thus wouldn't pick it up to read it.

I suppose the fact that you are here now, reading it, proves him wrong.

I was a first-time author who knew nothing about the publishing industry. I had talked to a publisher a few years before who seemed interested in publishing the book, but when I reached out with a draft, he said they were already committed to other authors. So, when I found someone willing to publish the book, I jumped at the chance and trusted them to guide me through the process.

Little did I know they didn't have my best interest at heart.

They talked me out of not only the title, but the cover design that I originally wanted. I trusted them when they told me the book had been professionally edited (it was not).

The bottom line was that I didn't know what I didn't know back then.

A lot has changed.

Having been in the publishing business for years now, we updated the manuscript, had it professionally edited, laid out, and typographed so that we could re-publish it the way it was originally intended.

Ie hope this new version will help you on your life's journey.

In gratitude,

Michael Jenet
Publisher-Author

INTRODUCTION

I wrote this book because I had to.

I had been trying to write it for a long time—years when I think about it. I even gave a TEDx Talk about the basic concepts it contains.

At first, I couldn't decide how or what to write. I had been formulating the idea in my mind but wasn't sure how to approach it. I wasn't sure if anything I had to say was worth reading. My wife was the one who got me started.

She asked me why I wasn't writing the book. She knew, even before I did, that it was because of fear. I was afraid no one would want to read it. I was afraid that I had nothing original to say. I was afraid that this idea was old hat, and that everyone knew it already.

In her own way, my wife slapped me in the face (not literally) and told me she had never heard of the things I talked about. Then she asked me why I thought everyone else had heard of them. She pointed out that most books are not based on new ideas. With the information age and the internet, almost everything is based on something else, which is based on something else, and so on. "Besides," she said, "aren't you the one saying that the true 'secrets' to success have been around forever?"

Of course, I still had another fear to serve up, but before I could gather my thoughts, she dished out one other simple truth.

Even if I had nothing new to say (a notion she disagreed with), no one could say it the way I did. Maybe, she pointed out, my book was supposed to reach those who had not yet cottoned on to the ideas and principles I shared, and the only way they could do so was if I told them by writing in my own way.

So, I began writing. I found it difficult when I started. I wanted to explain my ideas simply so that anyone reading this book could grasp them, whether they were lifelong students of success or beginners.

I soon found, however, that my writing was . . . well, boring. It sounded like every other business or self-improvement book on the shelf. That is not what I wanted; it wasn't me.

I don't talk about this stuff behind a lectern while reading from a script. When I teach the concept of MOTIVESTIONS, I'm excited about it. I walk around waving my arms. My voice becomes passionate, and the more I talk, the more excited I become. So, writing it down in a lecture style drove me crazy.

It just wasn't me.

I finally decided that I would not "write" this book. I was going to *speak* it. (That ought to come across interestingly in the audio version.)

What I mean is that I am going to have a conversation with you, just as though we were sitting down together over a cup of coffee.

I'm sure an editor who looks at this will get a headache just from the style of writing, never mind the sentence structures; I don't care. I want to communicate as if I were sitting with you, and we were discussing the points in the book face to face. This book isn't something I want you to read and then put on the shelf and forget about. It's something I want you to absorb. My hope for you is that this book will become a part of your everyday life—a resource you can turn to again and again as you grow and move on to living your best life.

This would be a good time for me to say that much of what you will read is based on my study and knowledge of human behavior, combined with my own experiences and beliefs. I hope this book will help you realize that achieving your dreams and goals is possible—and enjoying the process along the way is not only possible but necessary.

If what I say makes sense to you, great. However, if something I say doesn't sit right, that's okay too. Take what you want from these pages and apply them to your life. The stuff that doesn't resonate with you may not apply to you, or it may not apply to you because of where you are on your journey. That's fine. I want this book to be a resource you can return to as you continue to grow in life. Chances are, when you reread it, those pieces that spoke to you the last time may or may not still apply to you, and perhaps concepts that did not seem to fit your life before will fit better now.

Think of it this way. Have you ever watched a movie or read a book, and then later, maybe even years later, you reread the book or rewatched the movie and there were details you saw or read that you swore were not there the first time? What about a movie you *loved* years ago, but when you watched it again more recently, you just didn't get it?

Why is that?

Well, it's because our lives change. Just like how your taste buds change, and foods you didn't like before, you like now—the same is true in other areas of your life. You enjoyed the movie the first time you saw it because of your life experiences and where you were at that moment. Years later, you have changed. So, many things that did not really apply to you back then do now, and you notice them.

So, I hope you're comfortable. Grab your favorite blan-
ket; get a cup of hot cocoa, coffee, or tea; sit in your favorite
chair; and let's get started.

I can't wait to tell you about the principles in this book.
They're going to change your life. Not just the big goals and
ultimate dreams of your life—though definitely those—but
the normal "everydays" of your life as well.

Come on, let's go!

Chapter 1
Life's Journey

Why?

That's the word I've been saying more than any other my entire life.

I was always a curious child, and when I began understanding the world around me, the first thing that didn't make sense to me was why things differed from one person to another.

Why, for example, was one couple happy and another miserable? Why was one person more successful than another when they both had similar, if not identical, opportunities? Why did different parts of a country thrive while other parts struggled?

The more I asked why, the more confused I got. There seemed to be no rhyme or reason for the answers to my questions.

As a young adult, I was introduced to the personal success genre of books, the so-called "self-help" section of bookstores. Today, words like "guru" and "expert" are thrown about like confetti, along with "success coaches," "personal

achievement," and "life coaches," to describe an entire industry created to help people live better, more fulfilling lives.

I devoured those books. I listened to tapes. (For those
of you not old enough to know what I am talking about,
google "cassette tape" and laugh.) I attended conferences,
and I studied.

I studied the so-called "Masters of Success." I completed
countless programs, made lists, set goals, wrote everything
down, and followed every principle, tenet, rule, and "secret"
that would help me live the life I wanted.

I admit this took a long time—years, in fact. Although
I achieved varying levels of success, like most people, I
also struggled and remained befuddled by the variation of
success—or lack of it—from one person to another. "Why?"
my mind screamed. I wanted to know!

Why?

The power of this one word has driven me to try to
understand human behavior—not from a scientific point of
view, with blind studies and laboratory research, but from
a simple approach through observation, reading, listening,
and asking a lot of questions.

When you boil it all down, "Why?" is really the one
question that gets to the heart of everything.

Why, for instance, are you reading this book? It's going
to sound strange, but I actually know the answer.

I know we have probably never met before, and yet I can
say with absolute certainty that I know why you're reading
this book, and I can give you that answer by simply using
that one powerful word.

Say you picked up this book because you want to achieve
more in your life, or you want to accomplish some goal that
you have. Perhaps you want a new job, a new relationship,
more money, or to lose weight. Whatever the reason, or
whatever goal or desire you want to accomplish in your life,
I simply ask you . . . Why?

Let's pick losing weight as a goal. Why?

You might answer, "Because I don't like the way I look, and I want to be healthier."

Excellent . . . Why?

You might think that not liking the way you look and wanting to be healthier is enough of a reason, but bear with me for a minute. Why do you want to look better and why do you want to be healthier?

You might say, "Because I want to live longer, and I want to like who I see in the mirror."

Brilliant! Why?

I know, it's annoying, but stay with me. We're getting there.

Why do you want to live longer or to like who stares back at you in the mirror?

Here's the thing. Ultimately, if you keep digging, everyone everywhere is doing what they do for the same reason. You don't want to lose weight because you love watching what you eat, counting calories, and exercising. You don't want to be healthy because you love limiting the amount of good food you get to enjoy, or because you want to spend some of your limited free time exercising. The real reason you want to lose weight is simple.

It's because you want to be *happy!*

That's it. That is the end to every single thing you want in life. Ask *why* enough, and ultimately, you'll get down to whatever makes you feel better—what makes you happy.

You want a better relationship, not because you love the agony and trials of dating or enjoy wondering if he or she will ever call. Or going through all the bad dates and the cost, time, and anguish of finding a partner. It is because being with someone who loves you as much as you love them makes you *happy*.

You want more money, not because you enjoy having pieces of paper with pictures of current or former dignitaries on them, or because you love looking at your bank account and seeing the numbers tick up. You don't even want more money because of the things it will buy for you. Sure, paying off those bills, upgrading your lifestyle, or even being able to give more to charities is something you might want to *do* with more money, but that is not why you want it. You want more money because all the things I just mentioned will make you feel good. They will make you *happy*.

You see. We're doing the same things in life no matter what those things are. We do things to be happy and to avoid being unhappy.

Sounds simplistic, doesn't it? But it's true.

Here is the really obvious part that most people don't realize. We want to be happy with everything we do. Every action we take during our day is an attempt to avoid being unhappy and to achieve happiness. As Tony Robbins puts it, we want to avoid pain and gain pleasure.

Think about it.

Now, I know what you're thinking. You're thinking that not *everything* you have to do during your day makes you happy, and you're right. There are plenty of things we must do, either personally or professionally, that we may not like to do or want to do. So why do we do them? Because we have to? Actually . . . no.

When you think about it, we always have a choice. We choose to do what we do because it gets us closer to being happy than the alternative. You brush your teeth not because you love scrubbing your pearly whites with little pieces of plastic, but because you would rather do that than deal with the pain and unpleasantness of cavities or, even worse, the potential admonishment the next time you visit the dentist.

We attend meetings we would rather avoid because if we don't, we could get in trouble or maybe even lose our job. We aren't crazy about going to the meeting, but it's better than not having a job, right?

No one enjoys taking out the trash, but the alternative is foul smells, disease, and unsanitary living conditions.

Every decision we make answers the question in the back of our minds—will this get us closer to or further away from our goal?—and our ultimate goal is to be happy and to experience joy. Maybe the action we are about to take won't actually make us happy in that moment, but it will get us closer to being happy than the alternative action.

It makes sense that we would all rather be happy than unhappy, and if happiness is the ultimate goal we want or need to achieve in our lives, then the question we all want the answer to is, How do we get it?

That's what this book is all about: how we can achieve that ultimate goal in everything we do. I'm talking about everything from super huge goals and dreams to the minutiae of day-to-day living.

My quest for an answer to this problem expanded beyond careers and fortune to life itself. Many people measure success by economic outcomes, social status, or material possessions, but genuine success is about how you live your life, not just the things you possess.. There is nothing wrong with having or wanting nice things, but that is not the end-all and be-all of success.

Now, let's talk about *your* success.

Most business and personal achievement books deal with success on a grand scale. Free yourself up to dream big, write down your goals, put together an action plan, execute the plan, stay consistent, don't give up, and go for your dreams!

Great. Perfect. Wonderful stuff. I am right there with you!

Here's the thing. I have read more books on success and personal achievement than I can count. I have attended conferences and events with amazing speakers. Each speaker taught me something or reinforced something I knew before. I learned a great deal from every book I read.

So many books and speakers focused on the end goal, the dream—that big motivator that we had to keep our eye on. The prize at the end of the rainbow of our life that we worked toward.

Don't get me wrong; I am a passionate believer in dreaming big!

I absolutely believe in setting huge goals and working toward them. Never settle for mediocre. Never shoot for the lamppost when you should aim for the moon. I agree with that wholeheartedly, but there was always something missing that kept nagging at me. It took quite a while, but I finally figured out what it was.

You don't have to be a sports enthusiast or even a fan of the rich and famous Hollywood stars to get a glimpse of what I was missing. Take any star or athlete and examine their lives. Maybe they're an Olympian, a tennis pro, or a member of a football team; whoever they are, they're working toward a goal. The gold medal, the World Cup, Wimbledon, the Super Bowl—whatever it is, they have their goal, but what happens to them when they reach it?

Some continue and try to do it again, but for many, the achievement was the goal. Maybe they'll write a book afterward or become a coach or trainer, but nothing compares to the exhilaration of winning the prize. They spent all that time training and working toward the goal, and once it is over, they often find themselves at a loss.

Movie stars, rock stars—the news is full of those supposedly at the top of their game, with plenty of fame, fortune, and notoriety. And what happens to them? They overdose on drugs, or their relationships fall apart. You hear story after story of how unhappy their lives are. Why? How can this be? They have achieved what they worked so hard for. How could they be so unhappy?

I realized the same was true of my friends. Many found successful jobs, married wonderful people, started families and had bright, responsible children, and experienced what seemed to be great success in their lives, yet so many seemed miserable. Why?

The problem is not with achieving our dreams. There are plenty of great people who write and talk about how to do that. With all the information available today, it's easy to find someone who has gone where you want to go or has achieved what you want to achieve so you can model yourself after them. There are plenty of tools available to teach you how to identify your goals and dreams and how to write them down, put plans together, and implement them.

It's not the result and how to get it that's missing; it's the journey to the dream that is the problem. We are so focused on the big goal, the ultimate dream, that we forget the point of it all.

Remember what we talked about earlier—that our ultimate goal is to be happy and to experience joy in this wonderful journey of life? As human beings, our nature, our instinct, and our built-in desire is to be happy and live in a state of joy. But being happy should not depend on achieving our dream or long-term goal. Being happy is what we should experience along the way *to* our dreams and goals. By being happy on our life's journey, we can also be happy when we reach our destination. Life is meant to be lived, not merely endured.

The often-used Latin phrase "carpe diem" tries to capture this, imploring each of us to wake up and make the most out of each day. Another well-worn phrase is "Live every day as though it were your last," which echoes this sentiment. We can all see the logic and wisdom in such platitudes, but how many of us can truly say we're able to do that day in and day out?

If you were ever inspired by a movie or a speaker who urged you to "seize the day," you probably woke up the next morning energized and excited about your new attitude and outlook on life. You may have been able to live in your newfound happiness for a short period—an hour, a morning, and maybe, for a few lucky people, even a day or two. But life is not a straight path to nirvana, with beautiful landscapes on both sides, warm sunshine above, and the soft sounds of singing birds to keep you company. Life can be challenging at best, and downright arduous and heartbreaking at worst.

I respectfully suggest that "carpe diem" has it all wrong.

It is a great idea, and I am all about the notion that we should make the most out of every day. The challenge is that for most of us, it is nearly impossible to start our day and end it without facing numerous hurdles and obstacles that distract us from, and often derail, our best attempts to make the most out of that day.

For us to truly make the most out of every day, we have to make the most out of every moment.

I think the real notion we should all adopt is "Carpe Momenta" or "seize the moment"!

I am not suggesting we spend each second of our day focusing on how we can seize that moment while ignoring all that is going on around us, or that we somehow pay attention to every thought in our heads and try to correct our attitudes constantly—that would be impossible. It would be like walking on a sidewalk and looking straight down as we put each foot forward to make sure it was safe to do so. This might eventually lead us to our destination, but it would take far too long, and we would miss out on all the experiences and the surrounding beauty along the way.

So, what do I mean by Carpe Momenta?

We'll talk about the answer to that question as we explore this idea I call MOTIVESTIONS.

To do that, we need to start at the beginning.

Chapter 2
The DNA of Success

Being *happy* means different things to different people; it will even mean different things to us at different times in our lives.

Take our careers, for example. When we begin our working lives, most of us focus on how we can make money and climb the corporate ladder of success. This is usually because we have little to no money, and we are starting at the bottom of the ladder.

As life continues, we earn more money, and our circumstances and priorities change. Perhaps we start a family or get promoted to a point where, while the money still matters, we focus on other things. Eventually, we start wanting that work–life balance. At some point we determine that it's not about how much money, power, or status we have, but how we can find work that is rewarding, empowering, and fulfilling.

Happiness, however, is about more than work, and for each of us, happiness changes not only from year to year, but also from day to day. I scoured the vast library of books I had read and reread them. I listened to tapes and CDs, attended seminars, and searched the internet to find the answers to how people find happiness, in whatever form they deem it to take. It didn't matter whether it was professional success, personal success, or simply lifelong success.

I began to see patterns.

The fact is that although an enormous volume of new books comes out every year on personal achievement, business success, and all manner of "personal improvement," the content has been the same since the first classics of these genres were written centuries ago. Don't misunderstand me; there's value in each new book. Different generations face unique challenges, and sometimes we need to hear the same message in another way in order to apply it to our lives. Providing the tools and knowledge for how to live successfully or work smarter and more efficiently—updated for today's society—is not only beneficial, but necessary.

I read the classics of the old masters of personal achievement like Norman Vincent Peale, James Allen, Dale Carnegie, Napoleon Hill, David Schwartz, Zig Ziglar, and Og Mandino. I also read modern-day experts like Brené Brown, Steven Covey, Anthony Robbins, Jim Collins, and dozens of others in search of the formula, the patterns, the makeup of how to achieve success in whatever form it means to each of us.

I wrote down various components and dissected each one until I could put it all together like a brick pathway that virtually anyone could follow. I called it the DNA of Success. I thought that if I could document the steps that make someone successful, then anyone could take them and enjoy the same success that so many have achieved before them.

I started at the end of the path with the goal of happiness. I asked myself, "What helps us achieve each step of the process?"

The first realization I came to is that the single most important building block, if you will, that determines whether we reach our goal, consists of our actions—the things we do that either take us closer to, or further away from, our goal.

It doesn't matter how large or small the goal is; everything we do will influence that goal, positively or negatively.

Once I settled this major building block—that our actions determine our outcome (regardless of whether we achieve our goal)—I began thinking about what determines or influences our actions. Some things were obvious. Fear, for example, has a tremendous impact on the actions we take—fear of failure, fear of success, fear of ridicule, or fear of others' perceptions. Every type of fear imaginable can affect our actions. Fear can slow them down or speed them up. Fear can temporarily immobilize us or prevent us from taking any action at all.

Another influence on our actions is self-confidence. Self-confidence, or a lack of it, can keep us from acting, causing us to take the wrong action, or it can simply slow down our actions such that our outcome is affected. Self-confidence can also drive our actions in a positive direction. It can help us overcome fear and propel us toward our goals, regardless of what we may be afraid of.

This leads to another determining factor of our actions: our environment. Our environment is determined by the people we associate with and by what we listen to and read. What about consistency? I mean, any action can affect our goals, but it is really those actions we take with consistency that make the biggest difference. Arrrggghhh!

I was beginning to see that trying to diagram this pathway to success was much more involved than I had originally thought, and this was just the first building block! I was already getting multiple pathways by branching off the action building block, and there were many more to go.

The more I tried to refine it, the more complex the DNA of Success became. I quickly realized that I could write volumes on each building block, with all the branches that influenced them. I concluded that this wouldn't work. My goal was to help people, no matter their background, education, status, or how big or small their goals were. This

DNA of Success was just too complicated to be of help or to easily understand.

I mean, here you are reading this book to find out how you can improve your life. You're not looking for a doctoral thesis on the molecular breakdown of each step of the DNA of Success. This needs to be something you can quickly apply to your life, and since I didn't want to create a new version of *War and Peace*—the success version—I needed to find another way.

I decided to pare it down to the essentials.

I wanted to identify the most common success steps that others have discovered throughout the years so that anyone could follow them, duplicate them, and become "successful."

I went back to the drawing board and started with the goal. Although the goal is happiness, I needed to find the steps that people could take along the way that led to the hundreds of goals that ultimately end with us being happy. Happiness is not so much a goal but a by-product of the many goals we achieve along the way. Thus, these steps needed to be universal. If I could find the formula, then the DNA that takes someone from beginning to end—whether their goal is to lose five pounds or a hundred and five; to make an extra $100 a month or an extra $100,000, or to buy a new sweater or a new house, the same principles needed to apply.

I took the same approach as before. I started with actions because the ACTIONS that we take—day in and day out—are truly what determine our outcomes, and those outcomes determine whether we move closer to, or further away from, our goal. I don't mean every little thing we do during our day, but it's our consistent actions, in terms of the work we do or the directions we take, that ultimately determine whether we will reach our goals.

This led me to ask, 'What really drives our actions?'

If you think about it, there are several things that can determine what you do (the actions you take). Your habits certainly play a role. Your associations with others play a part. Your surroundings, your lifestyle, and so on, but if you had to boil it down to one thing, if there was one thing that primarily determines your actions, what would that be?

The answer is your FOCUS.

It's what we focus on consistently that drives the actions we take. If you focus continually on something you want, whatever that thing is, and you think about it, dream about it, look at pictures of it, talk about it, and imagine yourself having it, the things that you do over time, either directly or indirectly, will help you attain whatever it is you want. You might not always attain it the way you thought you might, but in the end, you will attain it.

You want to find a new romantic partner? Sure, you can use an app or hope to bump into someone at a coffee shop, but if you truly want to meet someone new, you make that the focus of your attention. You will keep an eye open, hoping you might actually meet someone at a coffee shop. You will talk to your friends and do any number of things consistently (taking actions) that will lead you to meet more people, which will eventually lead to finding someone new in your life.

You want to lose weight? It won't happen unless you apply consistent focus to that issue. Then, your actions will reflect your desire to lose weight. Whether watching what you eat, exercising more, taking charge of your health, and so on—all these things require you to focus, deliberately and consistently, to drive the actions you must take to achieve that goal.

I was on a roll. This made sense. So, if we focus on continually driving our ACTIONS, what determines our FOCUS?

The answer is our THOUGHTS.

What you think about will determine what you focus on. Now, of course, you think about many things, hundreds if not thousands of things, during your day. I'm not suggesting that each one of these things determines your focus. What I am saying is that what you think about will *affect* your focus. Your thoughts, not just what you think about but *how* you think about it, will determine what you focus on.

For example, if your goal is to buy a house, you will need to think about what kind of house you want and where you want to live and then focus on that consistently. By thinking about what you want, you focus your mind on what it will take to get it, taking actions which move you closer to your goal.

You think about the type of house you want to live in. This focuses your mind in many ways. You can explore what kinds of houses are available. Your action may be to explore via the internet all the homes that fit your wish list criteria. As you think about, explore, and decide on some that look interesting, your focus leads you to call a realtor, which leads to setting up appointments to view the homes.

Meanwhile, these thoughts about owning a home may lead you to focus on your finances to determine what it will take for you to afford a mortgage or perhaps to get pre-qualified for a mortgage.

It is the THOUGHTS of owning a new home that FOCUS your mind on all the things that need to happen, that lead you to taking ACTIONS, both short-term and long-term, that will ultimately lead you to owning that new home.

OK, are you with me so far? Our THOUGHTS determine our FOCUS, which drives our ACTIONS, which lead us either closer to, or further away from, our goals.

I really felt like I was making progress, but I was still not where I wanted to be in terms of helping people (like you) achieve their goals and dreams. I needed more. I needed to find that missing ingredient in this recipe for success. Sure, I was boiling things down to simple, manageable components that I could explain, but it simply wasn't enough to give people the tools they really needed to achieve their success.

Certainly, our dreams and goals will largely impact our thoughts. Even our beliefs, our upbringing, and our environment will affect the things we think about, but as I dug deeper into the question of what truly determines what we think about, I realized it wasn't anything external at all.

Simply put, it is the CONVERSATIONS we have in our minds.

I can see you shaking your head a little. Aren't conversations the same as thoughts? Not exactly. Thoughts come and go in varying forms, sometimes bouncing from one subject to another, sometimes fleeting and sometimes prolonged. They can be random or about something specific.

The conversations, the internal dialogues of our minds, interact with and drive the thoughts we bring to the forefront of our conscious minds. Think of the conversation as subconscious and conscious dialogue, which tells us what thoughts to pay attention to.

We all have it, an internal dialogue throughout the day where we react to what's going on in our lives. We think one way or another about what happens to us. There are many strategies available to help drive those conversations. Some people use mantras or positive affirmations to help guide and control them. Many people will tell you that your self-confidence (driven by the conversation you have in your mind) is primarily a result of your associations and input—in other words, the people you hang around with and the things you listen to, read, and watch.

It seemed to me that I had found the major building blocks, the primary steps that anyone could take to find success and achieve their goals—large and small. Directing the CONVERSATION in your mind drives the things you think about most. Those THOUGHTS determine your FOCUS, which in turn propels your ACTIONS. When done correctly, this leads you to your goal.

CONVERSATION → THOUGHTS → FOCUS → ACTIONS = GOAL

All you have to do is simply repeat the process for every goal in your life. It seemed simple, something everyone could understand, and yet . . .

While the steps themselves seemed simple, I still didn't have the answer. Sure, anyone could follow this formula, but it still didn't answer that nagging issue of "Why?"

Anyone could use mantras and affirmations to drive that internal dialogue to control their thoughts, change their focus, direct their actions, and achieve their goals, right?

No matter what I did, I just couldn't find the answer to that most basic of questions. Why are some people successful while others struggle? The answer was, in every respect, the missing link to what I was looking for.

Chapter 3
The Missing Link

I just couldn't get away from it. No matter where I ended up in the DNA of Success, I kept asking the same question. Why?

"Why?" is a powerful question. So much so that when I am talking about it, I refer to it as:

$$Pinput \ (t) \ I_Q V_{CC} + Iout \ (t) \ V_{CC} \bullet Y$$

which is just a fun way of saying "The power of Y," or in my vernacular, the Power of "Why?" Asking that one simple question—"Why?"—will help you find many brilliant answers.

I kept going around and around the DNA of Success model. I kept asking, why did this work for some, but not for others? I searched through books and stories of successful people, looking for an answer to my question. How were they able to accomplish what they did? Why did some succeed while others failed? What were the secrets that they used to succeed? Why did *those* things help them succeed when entirely different things seemed to help others?

Then, there was positive thinking. Everything I read suggested that if you thought negatively, you should simply replace that negative thought with a positive one. Great advice. But how? I don't know about you, but when I'm being negative, it doesn't matter how much I recognize it; I can't simply stop the thought and replace it. If I'm really mad, for instance, I can't even consider the idea. There had to be something I was missing.

Round and round I went, asking question after question, trying to find the answer until one day, I figured it out.

It was my teenage son who helped me. He went through a phase where he loved wearing T-shirts with funny sayings on them. One of my favorites was one that said, "Do you believe in love at first sight, or should I walk by again?"

On this particular day, he was wearing a shirt with a diagram on the front and back—you've probably seen this on the internet.

On the front, it read something like this:

FINAL EXAM
Quadratic Equations

1. Find x

$$x = \frac{-b \pm \sqrt{b^2 - 4ac}}{2a}$$

And on the back of the shirt was the following:

FINAL EXAM
Quadratic Equations

1. Find x

$$\left(x\right) = \frac{-b \pm \sqrt{b^2 - 4ac}}{2a}$$

Here it is

Sure, the shirt was funny, and I had seen him wear it many times, but that day it all clicked. The answer to my question of "Why?" In fact, the answer to every single question I was asking—was not an answer at all.

The answer . . . was questions!

Now, I know you're probably thinking, "Wait a minute. The answer to a question cannot be another question. We were taught to never answer questions with questions, and besides, if you do that, you never end up anywhere."

True enough, but bear with me for a minute, because that's not what I'm saying. I had been looking for answers to all my questions when the answer had been there, right in front of me, all along. Just like the x in the equation.

The reason some things worked for some people, but not for others. The reason one person with the same background, same status, and same education as another would end up hugely successful while the other struggled. The reason some people achieve their dreams and goals repeatedly while others never seem to set a goal, much less achieve it. Every single "Why?" I asked, boiled down to one thing.

Questions.

Remember our simplified version of the DNA of Success?

CONVERSATION → THOUGHTS → FOCUS → ACTIONS = GOAL

What I'm about to tell you will work even with the fully fleshed-out version of the DNA, but we'll stick with this one because you don't want to read my version of *War and Peace*.

Remember, I started out with the question, "What makes people able to do what they do?" The answer I kept coming back to was the beginning of the DNA: that conversation in their mind.

Clearly, those who are successful can control, direct, affect, and take charge of that conversation. They can have a different conversation in their mind than people who are less successful. They see opportunities where others see challenges. They bounce back from failures faster and better while others simply give up.

This led to the most important "why" question of all. Why are they able to do it and others are not? In other words, why are their conversations different?

What I realized was that it wasn't a conversation at all.

I mean, it's not like you have two people in your mind talking as if they're on some kind of entertainment program and you're watching or listening in. What's really happening is that your brain is asking and answering questions at a rate much faster than any computer can process. It uses the experiences you've had in your life to evaluate, process, and ultimately conclude whatever it's working on by asking and answering questions.

Think about it. From the time you get up in the morning to the time you go to bed at night, your mind is processing. When you wake up and hear your alarm go off, the first thing your mind does is ask a question:

"Should I get up, hit snooze, or turn it off?"

Once you get out of bed, it's "Bathroom or wake the kids?" followed by "Should I brush my teeth first, take a shower, or do both together?"

Your day continues with a barrage of questions and answers, many of them dictated by the events in your day:

"Do I have time for breakfast?" "What should I make the kids for lunch?" "What is the quickest route to drive today?" "Should I speed up or slow down?" "Why is that car in front driving so slowly?" "Where is that file I saved last week?" "Should I have some coffee or stick with water?" "Did he/she just give me a dirty look?" "What should I have for lunch?" "Should I check Facebook or email?" "Why hasn't he/she texted me back?" "Did we take anything out for dinner?" "Do these clothes look good on me?" "I wonder if he/she likes me?"

On and on it goes all day. You are constantly asking questions and answering them. Your brain is the most powerful computer imaginable. If you ask it a question, it will give you an answer. Sometimes with certainty, other times with hesitation. Sometimes based on facts, other times based on your experiences and known variables. It will always give you an answer.

It's the questions that shape the conversation in your mind. Want to know what you think about yourself? Ask.

Your self-esteem, self-confidence, and perception of your self-worth are determined by the questions you ask.

Don't believe me? Try it.

If you're not very self-confident, then think about the conversation in your head. It probably goes something like this:

Q: Am I self-confident?
A: How can you be self-confident when you fail all the time?
Q: Have I really failed that much?
A: Take a look. (At this point, your mind begins to play the extended, unedited director's cut of all your failures, going

all the way back to that really embarrassing moment your parents put you through when you were just a toddler.)
Q: Do I have any successes?
A: Sure, but not nearly as many as these failures. Here, take another look. (Replays previous video, now in super high definition with Dolby surround sound).

Whatever questions you ask, your mind will come up with answers. It's these very questions that determine the type of conversations you have in your mind. That conversation will then determine your thoughts, which influence your focus, which ultimately leads to your actions and—voilà—whether you are moving closer to, or further away from, your goal.

Let's try another one. Say you want to lose weight. Maybe your conversation begins with this:

"How can I lose weight? I have tried every diet there is and even if I lose the weight, it always comes back."

Sound familiar?

Your brain, of course, will answer you immediately.

"Oh yeah . . . you've tried before all right. Remember that one time you lost ten pounds, but then gained twenty? How about that fad diet last year where you lost so quickly that you had to go to the doctor? And when you came off the diet, it only took you three weeks to gain it all back. You're never going to lose this weight, so why not simply enjoy your life? What is it they say? Be happy with who you are? Go ahead, have another piece of chocolate cake. You can always start dieting again tomorrow."

"But I really want to lose weight. Is there a way for me to lose the weight?"

"Sure. Maybe you can go to a doctor and have surgery; that sounds like fun, doesn't it? Or maybe you can get a nutritionist and eat nothing but healthy nuts and tofu? That sounds like a great time. Let's face it. Life's too short. Why not just enjoy yourself, eat what you want, and stop worrying about weight? It's not really *that* important."

It's all about the questions and answers. But what does all this really mean?

If you don't like the direction you're headed (as it relates to your goal), the way you feel about yourself, or the way your life is right now, simply ask different questions.

Instead of your previous question about dieting, how about asking, *"How can I lose weight for good and enjoy the process?"*

Or how about *"What are some fun ways other people have lost weight and kept it off?"*

Or *"How do people who like to eat stay healthy?"*

Perhaps even *"Who do I know that lost weight, looks good, and seems to eat normally?"*

Your brain will still give you answers, only this time, they will be much more effective in helping you achieve your goal. Remember your ultimate goal . . . to be happy!

Is it really that simple?

Actually yes, it is. It works in any area of your life, but don't confuse simple with easy.

It doesn't matter what situation you're facing or what goal you have. If you don't like the way things are going or the results you're getting, then you need to start asking different questions.

If you ask different questions, you'll get different answers, which will change the conversation in your mind. That conversation will direct your thoughts, hone your focus, determine your actions, and lead you toward your goal.

By continually asking different (better) questions, you will ultimately succeed! It absolutely works, and it works every single time.

You may have heard the adage, "You can't continue to do what you've always done and expect to get different results." That same principle applies to the questions you ask yourself and, consequently, the conversation in your mind. You can't ask the same questions over and over and get different answers any more than you can have the same conversation in your mind and expect to take different actions.

It is a very simple principle.

Want different results? Ask different questions.

What if you ask new questions and still don't get the results you want?

Keep asking different questions!

Look, there is no guarantee that your first "new" question will lead you in the right direction. Like everything else in life, you learn by trying—trial and error. The only guarantee I can give you is that if you want different results, you need to ask different questions. You ask a different question and keep asking different questions for as long as it takes you to move in the right direction.

Change is not easy. You have spent most of your life running on autopilot. The questions you've been asking and answering have been the product of the things that have happened to you:

"Did you see the way he looked at me?" "Is that car moving too slowly?" "Should I go around?" "Am I hungry?" "What do I want to eat?"

Most of the time, your external stimulus triggers your brain to reflect on its experiences and analyze (in the form of questions and answers) how you should respond to any situation. Taking control of this process—actually controlling the questions that instantly pop up because of the bombardment of stimuli we face—is no simple task.

You're probably thinking something like, "Are you saying that I must pay attention to every single thought in my head all the time? That's impossible."

And you would be right. It is impossible. That's not what I'm saying, but before we get to that, let's talk a little more about this principle of asking different questions to drive different actions.

It takes effort, practice, and consistency, but it will be worth it. When you learn to ask different questions, you become the master of your own life. You control your reactions, your thoughts, your feelings, and your entire experience.

As I dissected this DNA of Success and realized that questions were the answer, I tried to come up with something to call my newfound discovery.

If you look up the word "motivate" in the Merriam-Webster dictionary, it says "to provide with a motive." If you look up "motive," it says, "something (as a need or desire) that causes a person to act."

Aha! There it was. The word I was looking for—MOTIVE. When I paired that word with the answer to my question—namely, QUESTIONS—it appeared they went together. That is how I came up with the term MOTIVESTIONS.

When I talk about MOTIVESTIONS, I often tell the stop-light story.

I worked in a job that had a long commute—forty-five minutes to an hour during "rush hour" (a term that I have never understood, since no one can ever actually "rush" anywhere). It was one of those days. I was hitting all the red lights, stoplight after stoplight. It got so bad that I swore I was hitting red lights from streets I wasn't even driving on.

When I finally got home, I was infuriated. I walked in the door and when my wife pleasantly asked, "How was your day?" followed by "Did you have a good drive?" I verbally pounced on her. I started complaining about the traffic, the lights, and the idiots who should not be allowed to drive. I let loose a barrage of complaints about how the city needed to time their lights so that traffic didn't get so backed up; I was on a roll.

I was ranting and raving as though my grown-up tantrum would somehow change things. Not only was it changing none of the supposed problems I saw, but it certainly wasn't changing my mood, much less the conversation in my head—the thoughts, focus, and actions that would make me happy.

Never mind, I was angry, and I wanted everyone to know it. Have I mentioned how intelligent and beautiful my wife is?

She let me go on. She nodded and let me get it all out. When I finally stopped—mostly from being out of breath—she looked at me with her amazing eyes and gently said, "Maybe you're not asking the right questions?"

I have to admit, my mouth dropped open.

"Maybe," she said in her kind, calm voice, "the reason you hit all those red lights was to keep you safe during your drive home by slowing down your drive. Maybe, the reason for the red lights is so that you enjoy your journey home. Each time you find yourself stopped, you can take a breath, relax, and look around to appreciate all the beauty around you in this great state of Colorado."

Yeah, that pretty much shut me up. It was the perfect example of using MOTIVESTIONS to change the conversation in my head and help me move closer to my goal of being happy.

To this day, I no longer worry about traffic. If I am late and the traffic is bad, I don't worry about it; I'll get there when I get there. Meanwhile, I take the time to appreciate the beauty around me; sometimes, it's the mountains in the distance, the beautiful sunshine, the cute baby in the car next to me, or the dog with his head out the window and an obvious smile on its panting face. And you know what? My drives are a lot more enjoyable.

People throughout time have figured out that what we get is what we focus on, the old garbage-in, garbage-out philosophy. If you spend your time focusing on the negative, guess what you'll get more of? That's right, more negative. Research is happening all the time to understand our brains—what makes them work? Which parts do what and how does it all play in our lives? What we know is that our focus determines our outcomes. My mother often told me as a young boy that I could do anything I put my mind to, and she was right. If I focus on something I want long enough, hard enough, and with enough consistency—chances are, I'll get it.

Does this mean we need to control every thought that comes into our brains to hone our focus constantly on what we want? Good grief, no. That would be a miserable way to live.

The concept of MOTIVESTIONS isn't about controlling your life or somehow managing every aspect, every day, and every moment. When I talked about Carpe Momenta, I wasn't suggesting that you pay attention to every single moment of your day.

The MOTIVESTIONS approach is, like so many other things, a tool. In and of itself, it can't do anything. It's how you use this tool that will improve your life, or it will simply be something you know but never use, like an old hammer at the bottom of a toolbox.

The key to finding that balance of knowing when to ask different questions, to pay attention to the moments, to use this tool to help direct you toward your goal is quite simple, and yet, it is that last piece of the puzzle that most people never seem to find.

It's the purpose behind it all, just like how questions were the answers; it is the beginning at the end.

Chapter 4
The Last Piece of the Puzzle

How can you possibly pay attention to every thought that enters your brain? You can't. That would be absurd.

Which might invite the question (no pun intended) of why I've been talking about questions and taking control of your thoughts. So how does it all work? I'm glad you asked.

I asked the same thing as I worked through my DNA of Success model. I realized that the answer to this question was in the problem I was trying to solve.

In fact, this one thing eludes most people who study personal achievement. If you take any topic and break it down—let's say affirmations—you'll once again find that it works for some people, but not others. Why?

What about goal setting? Same thing. Visioning or vision boarding? Yep.

Just about anything you can think of in the personal achievement field will work for some and not for others. The same is true of taking control of the questions that come into your mind.

However, what if I told you that one thing applies to each one of these areas, including questions, and it is the key to their success?

Well, hold on to your hat because here it is.

Like I said, it was at the end of the solution that I found the answer.

What is it we're all trying to achieve? Happiness, right? And what is happiness? It's a *feeling*. Feelings are the last piece of the puzzle, the missing link I had been seeking during my study. You want affirmations to work for you? You have to *feel* how the affirmation affects you. Don't just think about it. Don't just read or say the words out loud; it's not enough. You need to think *and* feel what the words are saying. Let your body and your mind absorb the affirmations so you can internalize the emotions that the affirmations bring out in you.

You want to do goal setting? After you've set your goals, written them down, prioritized and set dates, and determined the first steps that you are going to take, you need to reflect on the goal itself. How will you *feel* once you've achieved it? What will your life not only look like, but *feel like* once you've attained your goal? How will you feel when you wake up in the morning? Will your life feel different because you've attained your goal?

Feeling the outcome is what visioning is all about. It's not enough to just find pictures and talk about what you want. If you don't focus your mind to such an extent that you feel what it will be like to be, do, or have whatever your goal is, chances are that it won't be enough.

And yes, the same is true for asking the right questions. When you ask the right questions and change the conversation to direct your thoughts and your focus . . . your actions will have more impact if you feel that focus in your entire being. When your thoughts cause you to get a tingling feeling of excitement deep inside; when your focus is so bright, so intense, so clear, and so complete that you can almost taste whatever it is you want. When you can almost smell it, touch it, see it, *feel* it, and not just *think* it . . . then, and only then, will your actions start to consistently move in the direction you want them to go.

OK, so now you're nodding your head a little. It makes sense, and perhaps you're starting to understand how all these things fit together, but what does this have to do with knowing which moments to pay attention to and which ones to ignore? After all, research in 2020 by Julie Tseng and Jordan Poppenk referenced in an article for nature.com shows that we have about 6,200 thoughts a day. There's simply no way, with what you have going on in your life, that you could possibly analyze, reflect on, and process all those thoughts—let alone determine which questions led to them and what you should change in those questions to elicit different thoughts and thereby, different actions.

Everything we've discussed so far probably seems over-whelming, and it can be—I understand that. After all, we're challenging everything you know and how you've acted your entire life. That kind of change isn't easy, but then again, nothing worthwhile ever is.

Now, how about some good news because this part is actually pretty simple? Yeah, you're right, I didn't say easy. It's not hard at all, but it will take a little effort. The way to tell when to pay attention to the moments, when to use Carpe Momenta and know that it's time to ask different questions, is by simply paying attention to the way you *feel*.

You probably don't need to focus your attention on brush-ing your teeth in the morning—that's an autopilot kind of thing. What you want to pay attention to is when you notice that you're tense, worried, down, sad, frightened, anxious, or . . . well, you get the idea. When you notice that you're feeling a "negative" emotion, that's when Carpe Momenta jumps into the phone booth and puts on its superhero cape. That's when you need to use the power of MOTIVESTIONS and start asking different questions.

You'll know when you're feeling one of these negative emotions because your physiology will tell you. When you feel your shoulders tense, you frown, or your breathing comes in short, rapid bursts even though you're not moving, these are all indicators that something is wrong.

Sometimes your physiology won't be so clear, or perhaps you won't notice it, so you can't solely rely on how your body reacts. The key is to know how you are feeling. Are you angry, frustrated, sad, despondent, lethargic, upset, irritated, anxious, or just downright grumpy? These are all signs that the questions you're asking are not getting you the results you are looking for. From now on, pay attention to your feelings—they will guide you toward what you truly want. By noticing how you feel, you'll be taking the first step toward making the changes you need to improve your life.

Let's look at how this works.

First, try to identify the exact emotion or feeling you're experiencing; focus on it so that you know exactly what you're dealing with. Don't just think, "I'm sad." Knock it around a little and try to pinpoint what you're sad about. Make a list if you have to, but get specific about what's bringing you down.

Next, it's time to change that conversation.

Look, it's your party. If you want to wallow in self-pity, then that is entirely your prerogative, but know that you are choosing to experience that. You can make all the excuses you want—who did this to you, why you can't do something, or why it's so unfair—but remember, no one has the power to exert their will upon you unless you allow them to.

That's right. This is all your fault. Sorry, I know that's not fun to hear, but it's the truth. If you let someone else make you feel a certain way, then guess what? You *allowed* them to make you feel that way. I don't mean that you made them treat you a certain way; you can't control another person's actions, but you *can* control how you react to their actions— how you *feel* about it.

So, if you're feeling a negative emotion because of what someone did or said, it's because you're asking the wrong questions. Don't like the way you feel? Ask a different question, and another one, and another one; keep doing it until you change the way you feel.

"It's not that simple!" I can practically see you throwing your hands up and dropping this book on the table or onto the seat next to you on the train.

Yeah, you're right. It sounds too simple, and yet, it *is* actually that simple. It may sound strange, but the key to that statement of "It's not what happens to you, but how you deal with what happens to you, that determines your success" is really about what questions you ask.

Someone cuts you off in traffic and your mind immediately goes to "What is that crazy driver doing? He almost killed me!"

Or "Why do they always have to cut in front of me?"

How does this conversation make you feel? Are you angry or anxious? Are you irritated and frustrated because of what's happening to you? What if you took control of the conversation in your head? If you did, you might hear something like *"I wonder if they're in a hurry because it's an emergency?"* followed by, *"I hope they get there in time and safely."*

Or *"I wonder what's going on in that person's life that's making them drive so erratically? I hope it isn't something horrible."*

Now, how are you feeling about what's going on? In both cases, you couldn't control what was happening around you; you had no control over the driver's behavior. You did, however, have complete control over how you responded to that behavior and how it made you feel.

It takes practice, intention, and a desire on your part to take charge of your thoughts. But doing this in little ways, each day and each moment, whenever we can feel ourselves become negative, ultimately leads us to changing the questions, living a better life, achieving more goals, getting better results, and experiencing more joy.

So, the key here is to pay attention to our feelings. When we experience positive feelings, when we're happy and ecstatic and life is going well, there's no need to delve deeper—we're on track. But when we feel negativity, we need to pay attention to those moments—that's when we need to dig deeper to find the root cause of those feelings and to change the conversations in our minds.

Often, the biggest challenge to taking control of our thoughts and driving toward our best lives is that four-letter "F" word we all live with . . . fear!

Chapter 5
The Anatomy of Fear

Ah yes! What would a personal achievement book be without a chapter on fear? You may well ask, "What could I possibly add to the dazzling number of books already written on this subject, let alone all the various "experts" and self-help "gurus" who have covered this most common barrier to success ad nauseam?"

Let's face it. We have all heard dictums like "Do the things we fear, and the death of fear is certain" or "Face your fears to overcome them." How about "Fear is just God's way of challenging you to see if you really want it"? Or perhaps "Focus on your goals, not your fear." Of course, there are acronyms like "FEAR = false evidence appearing real" and "FEAR = false expectations about reality." The list is endless, and each one of these examples is powerful.

We all see the truth and power of these mantras and acronyms, and yet we continue to fear. So, why do we let fear stand in our way?

There it is again, my favorite question ("Why?").

All these platitudes may be true and well meaning; one could say they are even logically correct. But fear is not about logic. Fear is an emotion, and our emotions—our feelings—are incredibly powerful. It's going to take a lot more than simply having a logical way to think about fear to help us overcome it.

So, how do we change the way we feel about something? That's right, questions! After all, fear is really nothing more than answers to questions.

What?! I can almost see you jumping out of your chair on this one. You know you have me this time because fear is something you feel, not think. It is most definitively a real, gut-wrenching, sweat-inducing, goose-bump-causing reaction—not simply an answer to a question. "Aha," you're saying. "What is your answer to that one, Mr. Smarty Pants?"

Um . . . well . . . sorry, but yeah . . . Fear is really just a matter of answers to questions.

Hear me out. Let's take a common fear like, say, you are afraid of failure. Maybe you want to try out for a team or a play, start a new business, apply for a job, or that most common of fears . . . ask someone out! Whatever the goal, you have a huge fear of failing, and it stops you from even trying.

Think about that fear of failure for a second and answer my favorite question . . . Why? Why are you afraid? To answer that, stop and think about what you hear in your head—that internal conversation—when you think about doing the thing you want to do. My belief is that you will hear something like this:

"What if I ask her out and she says no?"

"What if I risk everything and my business fails?"

"What if I try out for the play and they make fun of me?"

"What if they find out I am looking for another job and fire me?"

"How can I go after my dreams when I need to be responsible and provide for my family?"

Sometimes these questions are disguised as assumptions. For example, "He won't want to go out with me; I'm probably not even his type."

What your brain is really asking is "Why would he want to go out with me?" or "What if he finds out I like him, but he doesn't like me?"

Another example: "I don't have enough time to learn something new; I'm too busy with my day-to-day responsibilities." What your brain is actually asking is "What if I try something new and I don't have time for my other responsibilities?" or "How can I learn something new when I don't even have time to do all my other responsibilities?"

When you stop and think about it, fear is nothing more than your mind answering the questions you pose. Those questions sometimes presuppose that the thing you want to do will have negative results.

It's the by-products of the answers to these questions that manifest themselves as emotion. You feel that gut-wrenching feeling in the pit of your stomach because of the answers your mind is giving you, not the other way around.

Let's try another one. Take fear of the dark, for example.

"What if there is a murderer lurking downstairs in the living room that is waiting to kill me?"

"How can I walk around when I can't see?"

"What if I stumble or fall and get hurt?"

Logically, we know that the room, the house, or the area we are in hasn't changed. But now, suddenly, because the light is gone, fear raises its head, and we're paralyzed. If it were simply a logical issue, we could overcome it, but we must overcome the emotion, that feeling that was borne out of watching horror movies, having an overactive imagination, or recalling some traumatic injury from our past.

That feeling comes from the conversation in our head and, as we already know, that conversation is simply a game of questions and answers. Ask a different question, and you'll get a different answer. Change the conversation, and you'll change the feeling. Change the feeling, and you can overcome the fear.

Replace the typical fear-of-the-dark questions with

> *"How can I walk through this room even though the lights are off?"*
> *"What is a great song to sing out loud to help me get over my fear of the dark?"*
> *"How can I feel strong and empowered even in the dark?"*
> *"When in my life have I felt powerful? How can I channel that feeling right now?"*

The challenge we all have with our emotions is that when we are in the middle of experiencing them, it's difficult to *think*. When something like fear, sorrow, or deep anger grips us, it's difficult to refocus and think about asking different questions. Our emotions rule our minds and bodies in those moments, and to change that conversation, we have to be in control of our minds and bodies.

So, how do we do that?

One answer is to move.

Yes, move! Changing your physiology, the way you are sitting, standing, walking, talking, and breathing. Changing your physical state is the key.

Feeling lethargic? Do a set of jumping jacks and watch your feelings change. Sure, it's a chemical thing—the blood courses through your veins, your heart pumps faster, and pretty soon your adrenaline kicks in. Suddenly, you're awake and alert. Magic! OK, not magic, but basic physiology.

If you are having negative emotions, take a moment to realize how you are feeling physically, then change it. Feeling sad? Try smiling for three minutes. Go ahead. Try it. Don't believe me? Try this. Put a silly grin on your face. Fake it if you have to; that's OK. Just smile from ear to ear—a big old Cheshire Cat–like smile. Now, stand up, hold your arms straight out from your sides, tilt your head back, take big deep breaths, look up, and smile your big silly smile. Now don't stop smiling, keep your arms out, breathe deeply—don't change a single thing. Now, try to be sad!

Impossible. Why? It takes work to feel sad, just like anything else. You have to slump your shoulders and let your arms hang like they weigh a thousand pounds. You have to frown, or at the very least drop your head forward with your eyes half-closed. You need to breathe with short, shallow breaths. There, *now* you can feel sad, but boy does it take work.

The point is, you must change your physical state. Do something outrageous. Run in place, do jumping jacks, spin around with your arms out, go lie on the grass and look at the sky or the stars.

Breathing is also an excellent way to change your physiology, especially if you're upset, nervous, or frustrated. Most of us don't breathe correctly when we're in a heightened state, and by changing the way you breathe, you can instantly change the way you're feeling, which will allow you to change your thoughts. Try this the next time you're feeling some type of strong negative emotion. Take a deep breath and let it out. Now, take another slow deep breath until you have completely filled up your lungs, and then hold it. The idea is that while you take the breath in, you count how many seconds it took to take that full, deep breath. Let's say it took you six seconds to fill up your lungs. Hold your breath for roughly three times that length of time. If it took you six seconds, hold your breath for eighteen seconds. Now, slowly exhale for twice as long as it took you to inhale. Again, if it took you six seconds to take your breath in, hold it for eighteen, and then let it out, bit by bit, for twelve. Once you have let out all the air in your lungs, take another deep breath and let it out quickly. Repeat the process five to ten times, depending on how long you take to let go of that bad feeling.

It may seem simple to just change your breathing; after all, you're breathing all the time, right? Yes, but how you breathe matters, and when you're not breathing in a way that fully oxygenates your body, it can have a big impact on how you feel. So, next time you start to feel something negative, try that breathing exercise and see how quickly that feeling goes away.

Change yourself physically, and whatever feeling you have will change as well. Of course, unless you can continually change your physiology, that feeling won't change forever—that's OK. It doesn't have to. All you need to do is change your state for long enough that you can focus on the questions that got you into that state in the first place, and then change those questions. Once you have rid yourself of the fear, anger, sadness, hurt, or whatever emotion you are trying to overcome, you can gain control of your mind. Think about what kind of feeling you want to have, and then change your conversation to better achieve that state of mind.

Here are some better questions to ask in the situations we talked about earlier.

> *Can I have fun asking her out regardless of her answer?*
>
> *What is a creative way to make my resume stand out that would be fun to play with?*
>
> *How can I remember that although they are interviewing me, I am also interviewing them to see if this is a job that I want?*
>
> *What if my business idea succeeds? How will that make me feel?*
>
> *If I risk everything and it doesn't turn out the way I had hoped, is it still possible for me to enjoy and survive that experience?*

It truly comes down to the questions.

Once, my wife was at a coffee shop and overheard a conversation as a new employee began his shift. A fellow employee asked, "Are you ready for your day?"

Most of us—when asked that question—instantly begin thinking through the day ahead of us and what has happened to us already. We do this in a fraction of a millisecond, as our computer brain processes this at lightning speed. We add this to how we're feeling physically and mentally, and more often than not, we come up with data that is hardly uplifting. So, many of us would answer with a bland "I suppose" or "Sure" at best, and at worst, something like "I can't wait for this day to be over" or "Let's just get this over with."

This man, however, had a completely different conversation going on in his head because his answer was one of the best I've ever heard.

His answer was, "The question is not if I am ready for my day. The question is, is the day ready for *me*?"

Bam! I *love* that.

Think about how that answer made him feel. I bet he felt powerful, full of energy, and ready to tackle whatever came his way. It's better to put ourselves into that state than to slump our shoulders, look down at the ground, and mumble, "Let's just get this over with."

Feelings! They are what you need to pay attention to so that you can ensure you're moving in the right direction. This is what you are ultimately trying to achieve—that powerful emotion of joy. And this is also the secret key to every step along the way—feeling your way to the attainment of your goals and feeling the thoughts, questions, and answers in your mind as you navigate the world around you. Using your feelings, your emotions, will help you overcome that.

There is, however, a set of emotions that are even worse than fear; they're the worst emotions of them all. They are the only feelings that MOTIVESTIONS cannot help you with—at least not at first.

Chapter 6
The Pit of Despair

For anyone who is a fan of the book and movie The Princess Bride, you'll understand the reference when I call this set of emotions the "Pit of Despair."

There are times in our lives that are simply shattering. Perhaps your significant other just left you, or you were laid off after years of faithful service to a company. Maybe you were mugged or robbed. Worst of all, losing a loved one can be truly devastating. Whatever the cause, you experience intense, piercing emotions of loss, sadness, or . . . despair.

To suggest that in times like these you simply need to ask different questions and all will be well again would be ludicrous at best, and horribly insensitive at worst. When life smacks you in the teeth, knocks the wind out of you, beats you down, and then kicks you until you are black and blue, you need time to process—for your own well-being, both mentally and physically. Time to grieve, mourn, understand, or simply rest and regroup. This is not the time to try to shift your focus; you need to deal with what has happened to you.

You must take the time—however long that may be—and handle what has happened in your own way.

I don't believe that everyone should deal with tragedy, loss, or whatever has put them in the Pit of Despair in the same way. We are each unique human beings with our own DNA and fingerprints. We each need to deal with the unexpected disasters of life in our own way.

There will come a point, however, when you have taken the time that you need. A point when you have processed, healed, or grieved and you're ready to move on. You may come to this realization intellectually or simply out of life's necessity to continue. Perhaps a friend or someone close to you has helped you realize that the time has come.

There is also a chance that none of these things will happen. In that case, you need to ask:

"How long?"

How long do you need? Again, this is different for everyone. It varies based on what has happened to you, how it has affected you, and what emotions you're feeling, as well as the intensity of those emotions. Whatever the case may be, ask yourself how long you need to process. There's no right or wrong answer. Only you can make that determination. Is it hours, days, weeks, or months? You get to decide, but it's essential that you set a time frame. If not, you may linger in the Pit of Despair far longer than you need, and it will make climbing out that much harder.

It doesn't matter when or how you get to that point, but when you do, you may find that climbing out is much more difficult than you imagined.

Maybe, before you fell into the Pit of Despair, you were a MOTIVESTIONS expert. You were a master of asking questions, governing your thoughts, directing your focus, and taking actions, which always led you toward your goals. But now, everything has changed. The Pit of Despair seems like an endless trench that you can't find your way out of. There are no ladders, no steps. Only a desolate tunnel with walls on every side and no way out.

When things are bad and you feel you're at the end of your rope—even though you "know" that you need to climb out, but you just can't find a way—at that point, am I saying that it's simply a matter of asking different questions, and you'll suddenly find yourself out of the Pit and in the sunlight again?

Actually, no!

Remember, our feelings are powerful things. So powerful that unless you engage them positively—to feel the goals you are trying to achieve—you will most likely fail to reach them. Our feelings are the key to success.

Those same emotions can exert equal power destructively. When you find yourself in the Pit of Despair, we're not talking about the run-of-the-mill blues or a bad hair day. Just as feelings can be the catalyst for success when positive, they can be equally cataclysmic when they're negative.

You won't be able to talk your way out of that kind of feeling using logic. You can change the questions all you want, but your heart will override the logic of your mind because emotions override logic.

Try "What am I happy about in my life right now?" after you have lost everything. Your brain will respond, "Are you kidding me? Happy? I am not happy about anything. In fact, I don't have anything, much less something to be happy about right now. You want me to point out all the things that I am not happy about right now?" And suddenly, you're off to the races and digging yourself deeper into the Pit of Despair.

What about "How can I get over losing my grandmother? I know she would want me to move on." Well, your heart and brain will team up and answer, "She was the most important person in your life. You can't just hop out of bed and pretend like she's still here. You would be slapping her in the face if you didn't mourn her properly. No one expects you to just get over it. How can you possibly focus on work right now when you can't even get out of bed?"

Once again, the elevator is headed straight down to the Pit and there is no emergency stop button.

So how does it end? If changing the questions won't give you the answers you need to climb out, how can you drive different actions? This is where you must be a little sneaky. Remember that deep down inside, you're ready to climb out. You do want to change the way you feel, but you don't know how. The pain and despair you've been feeling is so raw, so real, that you just can't seem to overcome it. And your brain is no help; it's tired and weak from working so hard to keep you going while you were in the Pit.

However, your brain is still a massive computer with all the answers. It's just waiting for you to feed it questions. Sure, it's going to reject the logical "let's get out of here" questions because it doesn't think you're ready yet. There's no way that it's going to let you try to change your physiology because it knows what you are trying to do. Right now, it's forcing you to conserve energy.

There is, however, a way.

If the Power of Why is the most important question I know, then this is the second most important one.

It's one I call "the Power of If."

Remember, your mind is still a massive computer. Since you can't ask it a direct question, especially when your emotions are running so high, you need to ask it a hypothetical one. Instead of "How can I stop feeling down and start feeling full of energy again?" because you know that your mind will find reasons not to focus on it, use the Power of If and ask:

> *If I want to start feeling more energetic, what could I do?*
>
> *If I want to get my life back on track and start looking for the positive things in my life right now, what would they be?*
>
> *If I were ready to focus on all the people who care about me and that I care about, who would be on that list?*

By using the hypothetical "If," you give your mind a way out. It doesn't have to defend the strong emotional heart that still hurts; it can focus on answering your questions because you don't really want to do anything. You're just asking, "What if?"

The fact is that by using this Power of If to ask the questions your brain needs to change your life around, you'll begin to change your life around.

It doesn't happen in an instant. Remember that Pit of Despair is not a small dip in the dirt; it's a deep, dark trench. But slowly, little by little, with each "what if" question, you begin to climb out. One by one, your brain will begin answering the questions, and you'll begin to focus on a future of possibilities instead of the present of hopelessness.

You begin with simple "what if" possibilities, and soon, you'll realize that they are more than just possibilities. At some point, you'll find the energy to change your physiology. A smile will return to your face, the bounce will find its way back to your step, and life will begin once again.

This is the Power of If. Yes, your brain will absolutely find answers for you, even during pain and suffering, when you allow it the freedom to detach by making your questions hypothetical.

> *If I wanted to be happy, how would I do that?*
> *If I felt like getting out of bed today, what would I do?*
> *If I decided it was time to look for a new career or job, where would I start?*

Remember, you can't do this when you're in the middle of anguish or at the beginning of something catastrophic. You need to allow yourself the time and energy to get through whatever crisis has befallen you. Life doesn't always go how we want it to. Sometimes, you just have to hunker down, face the storm, and hold on tight until it passes. Then, when you're ready—you'll know when that time comes—you'll start climbing back up. It won't be easy, but you know it'll be worth it. Life is meant to be lived, not merely endured.

Remember, Carpe Momenta is about living in the moments. If this moment involved having to face a storm, then so be it. Now it's time to get going before another moment passes. The Power of If is how you get back on the horse.

One more thought about the Pit of Despair. Anger is one of the strongest emotions that we can have as humans. If you find yourself feeling angry to the point that you think you're ready to climb out, then your climb will start with a ladder that is missing several rungs. Anger is one of those emotions that can derail even the best of intentions.

When you are feeling angry, using daily affirmations or mantras—simple daily sayings that you can repeat to yourself as you near your "goal date" for finishing the processing you need to do—can help you. These affirmations will help build those broken rungs on your ladder so that when you begin asking new questions, you'll have the strength and conviction you need to help yourself through this challenge.

You can also use affirmations or mantras as a tool to help keep you out of the Pit once you get out, or to keep you from falling into it in the first place.

The Power of If is not only a tool that you can use when you're in the Pit of Despair. It's also a great tool to use anytime you find yourself in a situation when changing the question isn't working.

I once had a manager who was stuck. He oversaw the largest department in the company, and they were heading toward a deadline that he felt could not be met. He came into my office and told me all the reasons why this would not work. How it was unrealistic, that it was impossible, and that his staff simply could not meet the deadline.

Most of the time, when you have a senior leader giving you this kind of feedback and you're the boss, you help your manager figure out what the right time frame should be. This particular manager was running the information technology (IT) department, and IT was my background. I knew what was and wasn't possible; I also knew that while this project might have been a stretch, it was definitely possible.

So, I tried asking him different questions.

Questions such as "How can we find a way to make this happen?" and "Is there some way to maximize resources to get this done?" I tried the old standby, "Since we don't have a choice on the timeline, how can we figure out a way to make this happen?"

He put up roadblocks to every question I posed. He wasn't a negative person, nor was he argumentative. He was simply stuck. He was in a place where he couldn't see a way out, and no matter what the question, he could only see that it wasn't possible.

Sure, I was the boss, and I could have simply said, "Because I said so," but that would not help him or his team. I needed him to find the answers so he could get his team behind the plan. I had to ask different questions.

I finally stopped the discussion and said, "OK, I hear you. It sounds like you feel as though this just can't be done." He nodded enthusiastically.

"Fine." I said, "Now I want you to humor me for a little while." I assured him I completely understood his position and his concerns. I told him I wanted to have a slightly different discussion, and then we would move on. He agreed. And so, I asked him this.

"What if it was actually possible?" Then, I followed up with, "Let's just pretend that this could be done, somehow." Finally, I said, "If it actually was possible, how would you do it?"

The questions completely derailed the train that had been speeding down the one-way track in his mind of "I can't," and instead he began thinking, "What if?"

It took a while. He started by saying he would have to add more resources. I answered, "OK, why? What would you do with them?"

That led to more thoughts and more ideas until eventually, he realized that maybe, just maybe, it was possible after all.

Sometimes it's not just about asking different questions, but about changing perspectives to help you get moving toward your goal.

Using these three tools—changing your physiology, using the Power of If, and saying affirmations or mantras—either separately or all three in combination, can be a powerful way to help get your life on track after a major setback or life event. (You'll find some sample affirmations in Chapter 13—MOTIVESTIONS Toolbox to help you get started.)

Chapter 7
Do What You Love, Love What You Do

So far, we have been focusing on how MOTIVESTIONS can help you with your personal goals, but what about your career, job, or business? Let's spend a little time talking about asking questions as they relate to making a living.

I know an entrepreneur whose motto is "Do what you love, love what you do." I love that motto. Lately, however, I have been running into articles and blog posts, even speakers, naysaying the idea that you should set out to do what you love. Some of them are harsh about it, attacking that concept and saying that going after your passion or trying to find a job doing what you love will simply be a waste of time. They add, you can't make money following such a course of action because it's based on emotion, not reality.

Others are less critical but suggest that although it may be noble to do what one loves, such attempts rarely work out. They insist that people who do so can rarely earn a living.

I even ran into a blog post that had me questioning my own belief that people should follow their passion and find work they truly love. I must admit I only read the post because the title really annoyed me. The premise was that doing what you love was the worst career advice the blog's author had ever received. The post began with the notion that we are all complicated human beings, multifaceted and multilayered, and that no one loves only one thing. The early conclusion the writer reached was simply this: How could you possibly pick one thing that you love to do when you actually love many different things?

I read that and my head tilted to one side, the way my dog does when I'm talking to her, as if saying, "Hmm, that's an interesting point."

The blog's author said that to find a job we would do for free was preposterous and added the idea that if you tell yourself that your job has to be something you'd do even if you didn't get paid, you'll be looking for a long time, maybe forever. So why set that standard? The reward for doing a job is contributing to something larger than you are, taking part in society and being valued in the form of money.

For a brief second, I almost bought into it. After all, it seemed logical. It made sense. Besides, the author was not really trying to say that you shouldn't go after your dreams, but that too many people feel pressured to do that. Instead, just be who you are because most of us find something we enjoy doing, right?

Wrong!

I respectfully disagree. I disagree with the author and all the other naysayers who maintain that the notion "do what you love" is preposterous, a waste of time, unattainable, et cetera.

Here's why.

When you hear someone try to dispel the notion of doing what you love, you must remember they are basing their statements on some false premises. The first is that if you do what you love, you will never have challenges, bad days, or ever be unhappy again. But nothing is perfect, and that includes work. You will have bad days. Even if you start your own business—because it has always been your passion—not every single facet of what you do will be something that you love. You may love the "job" of your business, whether it's cooking in your own restaurant, making your own wine or beer, designing websites, fixing engines, practicing law; whatever your "thing" is, you may love that aspect of your job. It is unlikely, however, that you will also love doing the accounting, paying the bills, cleaning the kitchen, dealing with unhappy clients, unclogging the toilet, filing your business taxes, finding the right location, moving . . . the list goes on. These are all parts of the job, but here's the point. Wouldn't you much rather have to deal with those things doing something you love than doing something you dislike?

Another false premise is that you are supposed to find what you love to do, start doing it, and then your life will be complete. One thing I agree with is that we are complex creatures. As human beings, we are constantly growing; our tastes for music and food, for what is important to us, change at varying stages in our lives. What I thought was important to me in my twenties was no longer that important to me when I reached my thirties. It changed yet again when I entered my forties, and so on.

Who said that if you find something you love and start doing it, then you have to do that for the rest of your life? Who's saying that something you are passionate about today, you will still be passionate about tomorrow? The point is that if you are passionate about it today, then you should endeavor to find a career that fulfills that passion for you in some way. Recognize that while it is possible you will remain passionate about it for the rest of your life, it is equally possible that your passions will change. At some point, you may sell off that endeavor and start another one.

Much of the arguments against "doing what you love" are based on the notion that people who go after their dream job will end up losing everything they have; thus, the goal is to find a practical job, something that will afford you the type of life you want to live rather than allow you to do the kind of work you would love to do.

Now, to be fair, this argument is often caveated with the notion that your work should contribute to society or your community. A noble sentiment, but again, I would argue that the premise is wrong. There is no law stating that if you go after your dreams in terms of a career, then you will lose everything you have. Has that happened? Absolutely. However, as with most things, there are two sides to every coin. There are also people who have gone after their dreams and been successful, some even wildly so.

Once again, I am left with the question of "Why?" Why do some succeed when going after their dreams while others fail? The answer is probably complex, but I believe that for some, it's because they're not really chasing their dream. They chase their dream job or career and fail because it wasn't their true passion. Oh sure, they wanted it, but wanting something and being truly passionate about it are two completely different things.

Others know their passion and go after it, but they aren't committed to attaining it. They want it handed to them, or after working on it for some time, they give up and decide that it's not worth the effort. (Which leads me back to my first premise: Was it really their passion to begin with?) Now, some of you will argue with me and say that you or someone you know did truly find their passion, worked extremely hard, gave it their all, and still failed. And I have no doubt that is true. Some people, despite their best efforts, are unsuccessful.

Again, there is no simple answer here, but sometimes, it might be because they didn't adjust to changing markets or didn't build a flexible structure around their business to enable it to adapt. Or perhaps the market simply changed, much like how the music industry did. For those of you old enough to remember the actual "records" of early music, you'll also remember how they changed to eight-track tapes, then cassette tapes, and ultimately, CDs. All those changes required everyone in the music industry to adapt. But then, digital music came on the scene and the music industry came to a grinding halt. No matter how well a company produces music CDs, the demand for that product has gone away. Those companies may have had excellent products with amazing employees, but through no fault of their own, the industry completely changed.

I'm not advocating that you should simply drop everything that you're doing and set out to pursue your dream job or business. I'm saying that the idea that one should "settle" for a job that gives back to their community but is based on the lifestyle you want (outside of work) is missing the point. That premise is, in a nutshell, "working to live," and it goes on to say that this is infinitely preferable to "living to work." I would agree . . . if those were your only two options.

The truth of the matter is that there is a third option, and that is to "live and work." I would add "passionately together." In other words, live your life and your work or career by following your dream—doing what makes you happy. Again, I'm not saying you should throw all caution out the window and start your own coffee shop today or what have you. What I'm saying is that our goal should be to find work that fulfills our passion and allows us to live our life with that passion, and ultimately, to do something that fulfills us and brings us joy. Then, we're not simply working to find a way to live the life we want; instead, we're living the life we want before, during, and after work. And yes, I believe that whatever it is we do, we should do it in a way that gives back to our community—it helps make the world a better place.

Ultimately, my reasons for believing so strongly in the principle that you should do what you love are simple. The first is that no matter who you are and what your dream job or business is, you will always work harder and experience more success doing something that you enjoy rather than something that you do not.

The second reason is that you will not achieve your goal of happiness if you are doing something that you aren't passionate about.

You may not be miserable, but I believe you'd be happiest in doing a job that you care deeply and passionately about.

The third, and perhaps most compelling reason of all, is simply time. Time is the one commodity we cannot buy back. Your life, my life, only has a finite number of hours. No one knows exactly how many hours, but we know that at some point, our time will stop. Yeah, this is the whole "make the most out of the time you have" speech but stay with me for just a second. Let me put it to you in a way that might make more sense than just the basic platitude.

Let's say that you work a "typical" eight-to-five job and get an hour off for lunch. That means you work 40 hours a week. Let's also assume that you have two weeks off for vacation, which means you work 50 weeks out of the year.

If we look at the total number of hours in a year and subtract 8 hours a night for sleep for every day of the year, that means that you are awake for 5,840 hours a year. Then, take your 40-hour workweek, plus 30 minutes a day for commuting, out of those 5,840 hours. You will spend 2,125 hours on your "job." That's almost 40 percent of your "waking hours." That doesn't count overtime or time you work at home, or on weekends—just the normal workdays.

If you own your own business, that number will probably jump to as high as 60 or 70 percent (at least, during the initial years of getting your business going) because you will work longer, have less vacation, and often work on weekends.

Why on earth would you want to spend a minimum of 40 percent (and possibly up to two-thirds) of your waking hours doing something you don't really want to do?

Think of it this way. If I told you I was going to give you a $100 in cash every day, but just before I handed it to you, I took $38 of it and threw it in the trash. What would you think? What if I took $65 and threw it away? This is no different. If you simply do a job because it "pays the bills," or it's more "realistic" than that secret dream you think about on rare occasions, you are throwing away over one-third, and probably more, of the most valuable commodity you have, and it's not money. It's time!

What does all of this have to do with MOTIVESTIONS?

If you're not doing something you truly enjoy and get excited about, the first question you need to ask yourself is, "Is this how I want to spend one-third, or one-half, or even two-thirds of my life?" Having trouble answering that? Try this. Imagine that your son or daughter is asking you if you think they should spend 40 percent or more of their time doing something they don't really enjoy. What would your answer be to them?

If your answer is no, then you need to start asking different questions. It's difficult to change careers, no matter how young or old you are. And if you are in a career that you are passionate about, but you aren't in a good company or position, again, you need to ask different questions.

For most people, this is scary stuff. When you're stuck in a job or career that you don't like, you're not only battling your dreams, but you're also battling fear of the unknown. Uncertainty of what might (or might not) happen if you try to change course is probably the biggest reason people stay in jobs they're not passionate about. After all, it's not that bad, right? Maybe you are making a decent salary, you like the people you work with, or you even find some of the work challenging; life is not that terrible. Except that every day, for at least eight hours a day (and likely longer), you trade that most precious of things . . . your time. Time away from those you love, time doing the things you truly enjoy, time with the very people, things, and places you are working for.

You're trading that time for something you're not passionate about. Therefore, if the solution is to change—if you need to find work, a business, or a job that excites, challenges, and meets your passion, and you have to overcome your fear—how do you do it?

The first step is to evaluate where you are right now. This can be a little daunting because you're asking yourself to face up to reality. This is, however, a vital step in changing your life and moving it toward what you truly want it to be. Here are some questions you can ask to evaluate where you are today in terms of your job, business, or career.

Do I get excited about going to work every day?
Do I feel depressed Sunday afternoons knowing that Monday I have to go back to work?
Do I look forward to the things I have to do at work?
Do I feel challenged in my job?
Do I think I have room for advancement in my chosen profession and/or at my current job?
Is what I do for a living contributing to my community or to the things that are important to me in life?
Does my career/job/chosen profession bring me joy?
Am I good at what I do?

Most of these questions deal with whether you're doing something you truly care about or enjoy. Maybe you're in the right profession, but not in the right location, or you need to start your own business in this line of work. How can you tell? Here are some questions you can ask to find out.

Is this company doing things the way I would do them?
Are we making as big of an impact as I think we could make?
Do I feel stifled by working for someone else?
Is there a way of doing my work differently that no other company does?

Is there a need for the work I do that isn't being met here or elsewhere?

How can I help move the company forward to new levels?

Are there opportunities for me to expand here, or do I need to move on?

These are just some questions you can use to help evaluate where you are right now. Most of the questions are simple "yes" or "no" questions. You can probably answer them easily, though some might require a little thought. The real key is to get to the bottom of this evaluation and, once again, back to feelings. When you answer these questions, you need to stop and think about how they make you feel.

I know, I know. You're probably thinking this is all getting a little too touchy feely. And really, what do feelings have to do with whether you're in the right job or profession? Well, everything.

When you ask yourself, "Do I get excited about going to work every day?" you can easily answer yes or no. But when you think about how that answer makes you feel, it's a totally different question. If you answered "no," how do you feel about that?

Similarly, if you answer the question, "Do I feel challenged or appreciated at my job" with "yes," how does that make you feel? See? It's not just the yes or no that matters; it's how it makes you feel that will truly determine where you are at this point in your life.

If being sad on Sunday afternoon doesn't bother you, then why change? On the other hand, if being sad affects how you interact with your friends or family and makes you dread going to work the next day, then maybe it's time to do something about it.

This is about your feelings. Not in the psychological "let's analyze your feelings and see how it relates to your mother and father" kind of way, but in the "we only have one life to live; let's make the most of it" kind of way. This is about feeling happy, fulfilled, passionate, excited, pumped, joyful, and all the other positive feelings you can have.

Again, I'm not trying to say that life will be perfect and that nothing bad will ever happen or that you won't feel sorrow, regret, frustration, et cetera . . . but I believe we should strive to feel as many positive emotions as we can, for as long as we can, so that we are truly living life the way it was meant to be lived. If we can evaluate ourselves honestly and determine that we need to change what we're doing, how we're doing it, or where we're doing it, then the next step is asking: What is it we want to do?

Chapter 8
Passion and Your Noble Purpose

Ah hah! Here it is. The Big Kahuna! The Grand Pooh-Bah of all questions.

During the early days of my career, I knew I wasn't fulfilling my dreams, my passions, my goals, and aspirations because I felt horrible. I was miserable, frustrated, and tired. As the saying goes, I was tired of being tired. I knew, both from my physiology and my mental state, that I was absolutely, positively, and unequivocally not following my passion.

The problem was that I had no idea what my passion was!

When you're young, say late teens or early twenties, your whole life is ahead of you, but you have little experience to draw from in terms of career paths or business professions. How are you supposed to know what you're going to pursue? How do you even know what you're good at? Perhaps you're going to a university, and you have to choose a path of study. How do you know that that is the thing you truly want to do, should do, or can do in terms of profession? Or perhaps you are going to learn by being someone's apprentice to learn a trade. You must choose something to learn that you hope will make you a good living and will fulfill you. It's a daunting task. Sadly, too many of us look toward something we have a mild interest in that will make us the most money. We often put less thought into our chosen path of learning than we do into planning our next vacation.

How many of us sit down, examine our lives, and think about what truly excites us? What we are passionate about and what thrills us? Do we really examine our goals and dreams, our passions, and our noble purpose in life to create a plan to attain them? How many of us follow our passions into careers and professions that uplift us?

I don't remember my advisers and school counselors having that conversation with me.

Honestly, I never remember any supervisor, manager, boss, or company I ever worked for having that conversation with me.

This isn't how things are done, and it makes me want to scream!

Why not try uniting our talents with our passions? Why not marry our goals and dreams with our abilities and expertise? Why do we spend less time thinking about life in terms of how it can fulfill our hearts instead of our bank accounts? We spend more time scrolling on social media or thinking about what to watch on television.

So, here I was, young and frustrated. I knew I didn't enjoy what I was doing, but I also had no idea what I wanted to do. Again, not uncommon for young people, though this experience is also common for those in their late twenties and thirties, even forties. Ever heard of "a midlife crisis," that point in your forties or early fifties where you look back and wonder what you've been doing all your life? The fact is that the realization that you aren't fulfilling your heart's true desire, your passion, and that you are not going after your goals and dreams but helping someone else achieve theirs can happen any time in your life. Sadly, for some, it never happens because they get stuck and never learn how to ask different questions.

Luckily for you and me, we're going to learn how to change things right now. It doesn't matter how young or old you are; it's never too early or too late to get on track. Whatever time you have left, now is the time to start living. If you are young, you have your whole life ahead of you, but you do not know how long or short that may be. If you are older, it doesn't matter how long you've been doing what you're doing; what matters is what you are going to do from here on out.

It took me far longer than I would have liked to realize I was not following my passion. I spent years being frustrated, knowing that I was not happy, but since I had no clue what I was passionate about, much less how to follow that passion, I didn't know what to change or how to change to it once I discovered what "it" was.

And that, my friend, is where we must start. We need to figure out what you're passionate about. The questions may seem obvious, but that's because you are now a student of MOTIVESTIONS, a student of your own life, and you now know that the key to learning is to ask different questions.

Here are some questions to help get you started in discovering your passions as they relate to your career. The thing to remember is that although the aim is to figure out how to match your career and professional path to your passions, your passions may have nothing to do with work. Don't let that bother you; answer these questions as honestly as you can. Whatever you do, do not worry about how you could do something. Pretend that I'm a magical genie and I'm going to make it happen for you. That "how to" part is not a problem; the only thing you must figure out is the "what."

I know that some of you will be unable to disconnect those amazing brains of yours enough to stop worrying about the "how to" part. For those that need to know the specifics, you'll be happy to hear that as you progress through the questions, the "how to" piece of matching them to your chosen profession will become clear. So go ahead, jump into the pool of questions. The water is warm and clean. The sun is shining, and the view is awesome. Let's have some fun.

> *What do I enjoy doing for fun?*
> *What are some things that I get totally excited about when I think of them?*
> *What areas of study really interest me?*
> *What are subjects I get passionate and animated about when I talk about them?*
> *What makes me laugh?*
> *What do I like to do in my spare time?*
> *If Bill Gates or Warren Buffett suddenly announced they were going to give me $1 million a year for the rest of my life, what kind of work would I want to do (after I paid off all my debt, bought a new house/ car, traveled the world, etc.)?*
> *Who have I read about or talked to and thought, "Wow, I would love to do what they do?"*
> *What is something I have always wanted to do but never thought I could do or would be any good at?*
> *When I think of all the different work/jobs/careers that exist in the world, what are the ones I think about that make my heart jump and my mind race with possibilities, and bring a smile to my face?*

Now, I wouldn't be a good MOTIVESTIONS teacher if I didn't remind you again that it's not enough to just answer these questions. I know you're tiring of me saying it, but I want you to stop reading right now. Go back to each question and remember how you answered each one, and then I want you to think about how that answer made you feel.

"Enough with the feelings already!" I can practically hear you screaming through the pages. I know; it seems so silly, but I promise you that this is vital to your success. When you answer the question about what you like to do for fun, I don't want you to just think of an answer. I want you to feel that answer. I want you to pay attention to which answers bring you the most joy. Which answers make you feel the happiest? Which answers to which questions excite you the most?

Only by feeling your answers can you truly discover what you are passionate about.

Passion is one of my favorite words. I don't use it lightly, and that's why I'm using it to describe your heart's true desire. I didn't say we needed to figure out what you "like" to do. I didn't say we were looking for a job or career that is "great." I specifically didn't say, "Let's determine what you're good at or find your hidden talent." All these things are good, but we want to find out what makes you happy, brings you joy, and makes your heart sing! We want to find that noble purpose inside of you, the one thing that you, and only you, can do better than anyone else, because it brings you the most pleasure by doing it. It doesn't matter what it is, but there is something within you, something you are uniquely created and equipped to do that includes your talents and abilities and is fueled and propelled by your passion! Your passion is the burning desire deep within your heart and soul. It's the need within you that only your true noble purpose can fulfill. By following your passion, you can quench the fire within you and live your life to its fullest potential.

Now, some of you may think, "What's the big deal? So what if I don't figure out my passion and noble purpose? Maybe I'll never actually find my passion and fulfill my heart's true desire, but I live a comfortable and happy life. What's so bad about that?"

Nothing. I'm not saying that you must do this. I'm not suggesting that you cannot be reasonably happy unless you do it. I'm saying that you will be happiest if you do it, and yes, you can certainly live a fulfilling life without doing this. There is, however, one other thing to consider, and it has nothing to do with you.

Your noble purpose, your passion, the thing that only you can do because you are uniquely you (uh oh, I think Dr. Seuss just took over my book), can only be done if you live your life to its fullest potential. If you don't, who knows what the world will miss? How many lives would you impact by following your passion and noble purpose? Unless you pursue these things, we will never know.

I've given you some time. Did you go back and reread your questions? Did you reexamine your answers and let yourself feel those answers? No? OK, I'll wait. Go ahead. I'll be here when you get done. Really, stop reading. It's that important for you to do this. I'm going to step away for a bit and come back when you've finished.

OK, how did it go? What did you learn about yourself? Have you identified some things that you're passionate about? Did you home in on some possibilities? If you are still not quite there, then you just need to keep going. If you're stuck, then use the Power of If.

> *If I wanted to figure out what I'm passionate about, what are some things I would think about?*
> *If I could focus on things that excite me, what would they be?*
> *If I'm sure I cannot figure out my passion, but I would love to, what are some avenues I could explore that might bring out my passion?*

You may also want to ask questions to get more specific about what your true passion entails. Maybe you have figured out the general area, but you're not sure about the specifics.

> *Now that I have the general idea, what is it about this idea that excites me?*
> *What part of it sounds like the most fun?*

*When I think about all the components of this, what is
the first part that comes to mind when I ask myself,
"What's the first thing that I would like to do in this
arena?"*

What's the most interesting part of this idea?

*What is it about this idea or what part of this idea
makes me wake up every morning and jump out of
bed to do?*

Whew! That was some serious brainwork you just did.
Well done! You just spent more time looking at what makes
you tick and what your passion is than most people do their
entire lives.

Now, just for a moment, I want you to forget about
your passion. Yep, forget everything you just did (just for a
little while), and let's talk about what you're good at. Look
at these questions and answer them thoughtfully. Yes,
you guessed it; I want you to pay attention to how those
answers make you feel. This time, it's not about whether
the feeling is necessarily positive or negative, but whether
the feeling is authentic.

What do I mean by authentic? Well, you're going to be
looking at your talents and abilities, and I want you to see if
the answers feel like they are really you. Is that a talent that
makes you feel like it's who you really are, or is it a talent you
learned because you were "supposed to"? Try to distinguish
between talents that you learned to do out of necessity versus
talents that feel like they come from within you.

*What is something that I do better than most people I
know?*

What things do I like to do as hobbies?

*When I have my annual performance report with my
supervisor, what are the things they point out that
I'm great at?*

> *If I could choose to do any type of work I wanted in
> any field, what type of work would that be?*
> *If a survey was taken of my closest friends and family,
> what would they say my greatest talents and abili-
> ties are?*
> *What situations do I feel the most confident in?*
> *What type of talent or ability am I using in those
> situations?*
> *What do I like to do that really gets me excited, some-
> thing that makes my heart race with anticipation
> and gets my adrenaline pumping? Whatever that is,
> what abilities or talents am I using?*

Are you getting a picture of the talents and abilities you already have and know you're pretty good at? I know we're all our own worst critics, but chances are if you think you're at least "OK" at something, then you're probably a great deal more than just OK.

So here you are. You have now identified some talents and abilities that you are better at than most, and you have spent some time thinking about what you are passionate about. Those are the two most important ingredients for the recipe that we needed. Time to cook up a future.

All we need to do now is ask the questions that will lead you to your goal. That goal will ultimately be the answer to this:

> *How do I find a career/profession that marries my
> passion with my abilities?*

Now, this part is not complicated, but you're going to have to do something critical if you want to get the most out of it. What you need to do is forget what you think you know. At this point, you are probably looking like my dog when she cocks her head a little to one side and whimpers as if her brain hurts.

What I mean by "forget what you think you know" is that you need to answer these questions like a child. Remember when you were a child? Anything was possible. You could imagine all sorts of things and reality had nothing to do with it. Well, that's the thinking you need to do here. Forget what you think you know about what is and isn't possible, and answer these questions as though you were a child again.

If I were given the task of creating a job description for something that married my passion with my talents/abilities, what would that job description be?

How long of a list can I come up with for all the careers/jobs that involve my passion?

How many people can I name that I have heard of (through the internet or TV—not necessarily people I know) who use what I'm passionate about in their daily lives? What ability/talent do I have that would allow me to add value to how one of those people does their job?

When I think about my greatest talent/ability, what are three ways I could put that talent/ability to use that would involve my passion?

Who are the most successful people in the field of my passion?

Who are the people with my talents/abilities who have been able to use them in their professions? What can I learn from them?

What do my passion and my talents/abilities have in common?

Did you revert to your childhood to answer those questions? Did you allow yourself to dream a little and come up with answers that weren't surrounded by choruses of "that's impossible" and "that will never happen"? If you didn't, I'm afraid you have to go back and answer them again. Sorry, that's how this works. No cutting corners or skimping. This is your life we're talking about. As John Wooden once said, "If you don't have time to do it right, when will you have time to do it over?" If you need to go back and answer the questions again, that's fine; I can wait. I'll be right here when you get back. Go on, do it now. Let me know when you're finished.

OK, so I'm going to assume that you have figured out at least some possibilities for marrying your passion with your abilities/talents. They may seem like crazy ideas—the best ones often are, by the way—and they probably seem impossible. Remember what Charles Swindoll said:

"We are all faced with a series of great opportunities brilliantly disguised as impossible situations."

What's important now is not knowing exactly how you're going to accomplish your ideas, but that you have them.

The trick now is to eat the elephant . . . Come on, you can finish this one with me. That's right . . . one bite at a time. The reason that so many people don't follow their passion, go after their dreams, et cetera is because it seems like such a daunting task—a mountain that looks insurmountable.

Only you know how quickly or slowly you can move toward your passion as it relates to your career. Maybe you're in a position where you can afford to start right away, or perhaps you need to move cautiously. Either way, you don't need to figure out every detail of your "path to passion" before you begin. Like the adage goes, if you wait until everything is perfect before you get pregnant, you'll never have children.

That fear of not knowing what to do is what holds most people back, but you're not "most people." Most people will not invest the time to read a book like this to better themselves. If life were predictable, then it would be boring. Think about it—if you knew what was going to happen every day in advance, what fun would that be? Part of the adventure in life is the unknown. Embrace the adventure before you.

The way you get past that "not knowing" is to begin immediately with small steps, which you can figure out by simply asking some questions (surprise!):

> *What is the one thing I can do today to take a small step toward a new career in the field of my passion?*
> *What resources are available to help me learn about career opportunities in the area of my passion?*
> *Who do I know that works in this field that I'm passionate about?*
> *Who do I know that knows someone or might know someone that works in this field that I'm passionate about?*
> *What company or companies do the type of work that I'm passionate about? How can I contact them to find out more?*
> *What education might I want to get that could help me move toward a career path that would lead me to my passion?*
> *What learning institutions can I research to find out how to get that education?*
> *Where might I be able to "apprentice" in a position that would allow me to try out working in the field of my passion?*
> *Who could I interview about working in the field of my passion?*
> *Are there blogs by people who work in the field of my passion that I could read?*

The bottom line here is that it doesn't matter what you do first or how much you do first. What matters is that you do something, anything. Ideally, each day, strive to do something—no matter how small—that moves you toward your passion, and if you can't do something every day, try every other day or every week. There is no right or wrong formula to this because everyone is different, and so are our circumstances.

OK, now that we have talked about what this means for you and your career, what if you like your job? Maybe you're already working in a field that is your passion. Let's talk about how MOTIVESTIONS work in the business world.

Chapter 9
The Business of Questions

Can MOTIVESTIONS help you in your business? Absolutely!

When I think of business in terms of people, there are three types: the employees, the supervisors or managers, and the executives—CEOs, presidents, and owners. Let's start with the employees.

As employees, we often receive directions without knowing the full reasons behind them. This is usually because we don't need to know, or it would take too long to explain every nuance of the complicated process that went into that decision. Sometimes, it's just because we have a control freak of a boss who is useless at communicating and just doesn't want to tell us—or am I the only one who has experienced that?

As employees, we often spend a lot of our time worrying, complaining, and being frustrated because we don't have all the information. We feel left out, kept in the dark. That leads to our feeling underappreciated, overworked, or taken for granted. As employees, we usually worry about money, and whenever someone leaves the company by choice, our first thought is that the company was not willing to pay them enough, so they took that other job.

Throughout my career, the exit interviews conducted by human resource departments have typically found that even though we would all like to earn more money, one of the biggest reasons people leave their jobs voluntarily is because they feel underappreciated.

As employees, when we encounter this situation, our first thought is "Yeah, that's because my boss never talks to me," ". . . is a horrible communicator," or ". . . doesn't care about me at all." My question for you is, when was the last time you took the time to talk to and get to know your boss?

Communication is a two-way street. As employees, it's important to know that it's as much up to us to communicate with our boss as it is for them to communicate with us.

Now, this doesn't mean we need to approach our boss and demand more information or complain more. If the goal is happiness—in this case, happiness at work—and if that happiness is about better communication and feeling appreciated, satisfied, challenged, and ultimately compensated appropriately, then perhaps a different line of questions is in order.

> *What can I do today to make the team/department more productive?*
>
> *How can I open up better avenues of communication with my boss?*
>
> *What would it take for me to show my boss that I add more value to the team?*
>
> *What could I do today to help my boss better understand what our department needs?*
>
> *Where am I exceeding my boss's expectations and where do I have room to improve? How can I ask for his/her help in those areas?*

Another challenge we face as employees is the monotony of our work, the loathing we have for some tasks that must be done, or even our challenges with other employees.

> *How can I get more enjoyment out of the work that I'm doing?*
> *Who do I know that seems to enjoy doing this part of our job and how can I learn their secret?*
> *What is one positive aspect about this part of my job?*
> *Is there a way to make a game out of this task, even if it's only a game that I am playing, like trying to break my best time for getting it done?*
> *What is one good quality about the employee I have the most challenges with? How might I be able to help this employee understand my point of view? What might help me understand theirs so we can figure out a solution?*

Finally, as employees, there is one problem we face that affects everyone. This is not solely an employee problem, but a people problem. We don't really know how to listen. When someone is talking to us, whether it's a coworker, our boss, a client, a vendor, whoever, we tend to only superficially hear what they are saying. Instead of listening, we formulate our own response before they have finished speaking.

One of the greatest skills you can learn, especially when you are starting out at the bottom of that ladder of success, is to become an exceptional listener. I won't lie to you; it's extremely difficult. Our nature as human beings is very self-focused, and when someone is talking to us, our mind's natural inclination is to think of what we're going to say as soon as that person has finished. Some of us—you know who you are—can't wait until the other person finishes speaking before beginning with our own answers or stories.

Questions can help you cultivate this "exceptional listener" skill.

Try this the next time you're talking to someone. As they begin speaking, ask yourself these questions:

> *How can I give them my complete attention until they have finished talking?*
> *What can I do to keep my eyes from wandering away while they are talking?*
> *What are the important points they are communicating to me?*
> *What can I learn from this conversation?*

By asking a few simple questions at the beginning of the conversation and anytime you feel your mind wander or formulate a response, you can focus on what your conversation partner is saying and ensure that you're truly listening to them. Listening skills take practice and are among the most important skills you could ever learn in life, both personally and professionally.

Next, let's see how questions can help supervisors and managers. Being in management or in a supervisory position involves several challenges. On the one hand, those of us in management are employees with a boss of our own. All the issues that employees face and the questions that can help them also apply to us. On the other hand, we have employees who report to us, and there are unique challenges we must face with them as well.

As I mentioned before, poor listening is a problem applicable to people in general, not only employees. It's equally vital as a supervisor or manager that you become adept at listening. Using the same questions to ensure that you are truly listening when your employees are talking to you is a vital step. Everyone wants to be heard. Not simply mollified, but truly heard for their ideas, feedback, or concerns. Make sure you become an expert listener so your employees will feel comfortable coming to you with their challenges and ideas.

To improve your listening, you need to learn how to pay attention to your employees, learn about them, and see what makes them "tick." Here are some questions that can help you:

> *What are my employees' greatest strengths?*
> *How can I help them use those strengths to their advantage?*
> *What is it like to be in their shoes in this situation? How must they be feeling right now?*
> *What are they really trying to say, apart from what they think I want to hear?*
> *How can I help my employees find the solution without telling them what it is so they can develop their potential?*
> *What do I really know about my employees' goals and dreams?*
> *How can I learn more about what my employees really need and want?*
> *How can I motivate the team to all pull together to accomplish our goal?*

One consequence of moving into a supervisory or management role is that you instantly get assigned to meetings. Sometimes, these are meetings over which you have no control; you're simply a participant. In other cases, you preside over meetings in order to manage your staff, team, or department.

I don't know about you, but I hate meetings. Sure, they are necessary, and some can be very productive. What bugs me, though, is how much time they waste. Now, there are many books out there on how to become more efficient in meetings and how to run effective meetings, so I'm not going to address that topic here. Instead, I want to talk about what it's like to be a participant, whether or not the meeting is one that you have control over.

My point is, what are you going to get out of the meetings you attend? You may or may not preside over or control the meeting, but you do have control over how you interact during it.

If you ask yourself a basic question before you go into a meeting, it will help your focus and interaction.

What is my goal for this meeting?

What do you want to get out of it? This is a powerful question to ask. For instance, let's go back to before you got your job. You had to interview to get this job, and an interview is really nothing more than a meeting. It's usually a nerve-wracking, tense, and difficult meeting, but it's a meeting, nonetheless.

For most people, the answer to "What is my goal for this meeting?" would seem obvious. You want the job. OK, but try a different way of looking at it. When you interview for a position, most people forget that, although the interviewer asks most of the questions, you should also interview them. That's right. You need to interview them. They represent the company you will trade your valuable time to in exchange for compensation. Don't you think it's worth learning about the company and seeing if it's a good match for you?

Remember that barista who said the question was not whether he was ready for his day, but rather, was the day ready for him? Well, this is the same thing. The question is not simply "Am I the right person for this company," but "Is this company right for me?"

So, the better answer to the question "What is my goal for this meeting?" is about far more than getting a job. The answer probably includes many things. My goal might include:

- Making sure they learn enough about me to see that I am the best candidate for this position.

- Making good eye contact and smiling throughout the interview. Staying relaxed and being myself so they get a better idea of who I am.
- Learning about the company to see if it's somewhere that I would be proud to work.
- Learning about potential advancement opportunities for the future.
- Finding out what the company's goals and strategies are and how I would fit into them.

Interviews are just one example of meetings, and they are highly personal. Most meetings we attend involve other people and usually cover a wide range of topics. By asking yourself beforehand what your goal is or what you want to achieve, you set the tone for your behavior during that meeting.

Sometimes, it's a good idea to write down your goal or expected outcome at the top of your notepad to remind yourself of what you're hoping to achieve. By focusing on what it is you want, your actions during the meeting will help you stay on track.

Hmm . . . that sounds familiar, doesn't it?

During the meeting, especially if the topic is difficult or one in which other participants find threatening and perhaps unwilling to consider, you can ask yourself questions to help drive the conversation:

> *What is the primary hurdle that's keeping them from considering the goal? If I were in their shoes, what would it take for me to get past the hurdles?*
> *How can I help everyone in the meeting understand and rally around the primary goal we need to achieve?*

Another challenge can be that meetings necessary for your position (which you're required to attend) are not always helpful to you.

In those cases, there are still a couple of questions you can ask:

> *What can I take away from this meeting that's relevant to my department or staff?*
> *What can I learn from how this meeting is being conducted to help me better conduct my own meetings? (Sometimes it's learning what not to do as much as what to do that can be helpful.)*

Of course, sometimes a meeting is just something you must get through—a painful, boring, poorly run, and pointless meeting that has nothing to do with your work, your team, or your department. In those cases, aside from trying to secretly play solitaire on your tablet, you might ask yourself:

> *What can I think about to make the most of this time?*

Is there a challenge or hurdle you are trying to overcome that you could spend some of this unproductive time working through in your mind?

The last question is this: Can MOTIVESTIONS help the business itself?

Let's look at how questions can help CEOs, presidents, and owners. While the listening skill questions and supervisor and management questions all apply to the executive level of a company, I want to talk a little about how the leadership of a company can use questions from a visioning perspective.

To answer that, let's start with some examples.

For years, hotels all over the world bought mass-produced, standard beds. Some higher-end hotels might have had nicer linens and pillows, but much of the improvements went to aesthetics, food, customer service, pools, et cetera until someone asked a completely different question: "What if people left our hotel more refreshed than when they arrived?"

This led to major improvements in hotel beds, such that when you sleep at a hotel today, you expect the bed to be even better than the one you sleep on at home.

Another example we discussed previously is in the music industry. When vinyl record–making companies saw technology changing, they became the first eight-track companies, followed by cassette tape companies, and then ultimately, CD makers.

But it was a computer company that asked a totally different question: "What if you could carry all of your music with you?"

Apple saw MP3 technology and capitalized on it simply by asking a question no one else was asking. A whole new way of listening to and storing music began, which ultimately exploded with the invention of the iPod and now exists on virtually every modern cell phone.

Marketing companies have known for years that finding a new way to market products, rebrand a company, or launch a new ad blitz often comes down to looking at something from different angles or perspectives. This often results in others seeing your business or product from a new point of view, but you don't need to hire an expensive marketing firm to help your business or product find more success.

You simply need to ask different questions.

If you need more customers in your business, then think about the questions you have been asking and change them.

Perhaps, instead of saying, "How can we improve our product for our customers?" ask,

> *What if our customers helped design our products?*
> *What if our product fills a niche for our customers no one else has thought of?*

I was at a conference where some marketing people discussed different ways to look at situations to get more creative. As one example, they used the Band-Aid company.

Apparently, the people who make Band-Aids, like in any company that manufactures a product, were constantly trying to make a better product. Their goal was to make the best bandage possible by perfecting their product using different materials, making them waterproof or to give them more airiness. One thing that was of particular importance was "stickability." Why? Because they were always asking one very important question:

"How do we get Band-Aids to adhere better?"

Their customers wanted a better bandage, which would not dissolve in water, allowed air to flow through to the wound, and came in various sizes and colors and shapes. But the company's research showed that one aspect that mattered most to people wearing their bandages was the bandage's ability to stay on until it was time to take it off.

The company tried various glues, adhesives, and methods of packaging until ultimately, they came up with a great product that people would buy. Customers, of course, always want something better; there always seemed to be a need to make the bandages stick even better. So, the question remained: "How do we get Band-Aids to adhere more?"

Until one day, someone in the company asked a different question, which completely changed their approach to getting the results they were looking for. While everyone else was asking, "How do we make Band-Aids adhere more?" someone came up with a new question:

"What would it look like if Band-Aids couldn't fall off?"

This question was still about getting the Band-Aid to stick better, but instead of asking the same question, they changed the focus by asking it differently. The internal conversations about finding a different glue or adhesive stopped, allowing the team to examine many possibilities they had never considered before. Asking a different question didn't change their goal. It didn't change the company or deviate from its mission, but it completely changed the way the people who were working on the idea thought about the problem. The result?

The Band-Aid liquid bandage! A spray adhesive that created a way to cover a wound, but without an actual bandage.

Brilliant!

It solved the question of how to cover a wound and have the dressing stay on, but not by the traditional adhesive bandage everyone had been focused on. And it happened because someone asked a different question.

One popular story is about the now familiar Post-It notepads. In case you aren't familiar with it, Dr. Spencer Silver, an American chemist at 3M, was trying to develop a superstrong adhesive, but he came up with a "low-tack," reusable, pressure-sensitive one. Most people would regard that result as a failure, since it certainly did not achieve the goal of a superstrong adhesive, but Dr. Spencer felt he had created a "solution without a problem." He didn't simply ask the question, "Is this a superstrong adhesive?" because of course, the answer would have been no. Had that been the only question he asked, he would have simply discarded the formula and tried again. Instead, he asked a different question (something like "What problem does this solve?"), but ultimately, he was unable to find a use for his adhesive.

Maybe he didn't ask enough questions, or maybe he simply kept asking the wrong ones. Who knows? It was one of his colleagues at 3M who asked the right question. Art Fry was looking for a bookmark for his church hymnal, one that would not fall out or damage it. When he heard about the temporary, re-positionable adhesive Dr. Spencer had created, he wondered (read "asked the question") if he could apply it to paper and use it as a bookmark. And just like that, the Post-it Note was born.

How often do we assume that the outcome we achieve is simply an outright failure instead of a potential opportunity?

Asking different questions applies not only to the business that you do but also to the most important assets you have: your people. In my experience, I once took over as CEO of a company in which the executive assistant came to me because she felt she was no longer needed. The previous CEO was the type of person who needed a "handler," someone to help him with tasks, appointments, mail, et cetera. I was much more efficient and didn't need to rely on her for those things. I also saw much more potential in her.

I sat down with her and asked what she would like to do. Her answers were fairly predictable; she talked about how she could help me more and perhaps take on some additional duties to help other executives and staff. She was a highly intelligent woman with a more diverse background and skill set than her current position indicated, but she assumed she was still an executive assistant, until I asked her the following question:

"What if you weren't an executive assistant? What would you want to do?"

The question threw her; she wasn't thinking in those terms. We talked for a little while and I suggested some areas in the company that I felt weren't fully used or, sometimes, not used at all. I gave her a high-level view of where I wanted to take the company. She said she wanted to think about it and get back to me.

A few days later, she returned with a proposal to start a new department, with her as the sole employee the first year. The goal of the department specifically aligned with her talents from prior jobs and the needs we had discussed.

Brilliant! Within eighteen months, she had grown the department and brought in additional sources of revenue the company had never had before.

Sometimes we get stuck because we're asking the same question repeatedly. What's that quote often attributed to Einstein? The definition of insanity is doing the same thing over and over again but expecting different results. Well, the same thing is true of the questions we ask. Asking the same question repeatedly but expecting different answers is equally frustrating. Change the questions you're asking as they relate to your company's goals. Look at your goals from different angles and different perspectives. Ask questions differently, and you'll soon find that you're coming up with different answers or even different solutions.

No matter what role you have in a company, you can use questions to help yourself, your team, and the company:

> *How could we better serve our customers?*
> *Is there a way to make our products/services stand out from our competition?*
> *What could we do to make this a better place to work so we can attract better employees?*
> *How can we make a game out of this project so that everyone has fun while we work?*
> *What are three ways we could increase productivity without increasing cost?*
> *How could we engage employees to help come up with new ideas for innovation and efficiencies across the company?*
> *What do our customers need, and how can we learn new ways to help meet those needs?*

OK, so that's all fine and well if you're an inventor or a marketing wizard. What if you work in a restaurant or you're an engineer? Perhaps you work in sales? Software engineering? The service sector? How does this idea of asking different questions work for you?

Let me answer that by asking you a question. Has your boss ever asked you to do something that you felt was impossible or simply unreasonable? Have you ever been given a task that you walked out of their office with, sat down, and thought, "There is no way that I'm going to do this!"

We have all been asked to make the impossible happen, to meet some deadline that looked unachievable or to strive for a goal that seemed out of reach. When that happened to me, I spent a great deal of time wallowing in self-pity. "Why am I always the one asked to do the impossible?" "Doesn't he know there's no way my department can do that in two weeks?" "Why doesn't my boss understand that when I say it can't be done? I know what I'm talking about."

In these situations, I analyze and reassess all the various ways that what I'm being asked to do is unfair, unrealistic, and downright impossible. I come up with ways to go back and explain all my reasons why this is simply not going to happen.

Of course, it's entirely possible that I'm right, but what is that going to do for me? First, I'm immediately stressed, I become anxious, and I spend valuable time worrying about things that haven't even taken place yet. All of this because the question I immediately asked myself was "How can I do the impossible?" and I presupposed it was, in fact, impossible.

What if, instead, I simply started asking different questions?

How can I look objectively at this challenge to see what possibilities exist?

And, of course, there is also the powerful "what if" version.

What if this is possible to do? What would it take to make happen?

Immediately, I remove the pressure of assuming it's impossible. I have changed an impossible task into a challenge (a great word to use instead of "problem") that may or may not have potential solutions. Sure, it's still my responsibility, but now I have options. First, it frees up my mind to think that maybe it is possible. This changes the way I think, much like the Band-Aid question. Second, instead of focusing on "It's impossible," I focus on "What if it were possible?"

Even if the result is truly an impossible task, I will have thought through multiple ideas—maybe even tried some of them—and if I have to go back to the boss and explain, I will have more data to share and justification why we could not accomplish the task.

More likely, however, because I'm asking different questions, I might find a solution I never thought of by simply framing the questions that support me rather than asking the immediate questions that limit my thinking.

I once worked with a salesperson who taught me an incredible lesson, a lesson I later found reinforced and expertly articulated in the bestselling book The Go-Giver by Bob Burg and John David Mann. There are many books and seminars written about the sales profession. For years, these so-called experts came up with various ways to "get ahead" in the world of sales. Things like "the art of closing the deal" became commonplace language. From prospecting and networking to cold calling and how not to take no for an answer, it seemed like each year, a new technique emerged.

The lesson I learned from the salesperson I worked with was completely different. Instead of the traditional salesperson, who focuses on how they could get the biggest sales or who convinces the customer to buy their wares, this salesperson did something radically different. He changed the question from how his client could help him to how he could help his client.

He didn't go into a meeting thinking about how he could get them to buy his products and services. Instead, he genuinely went in to learn what his client did. His questions were not "Let's talk about how and why you need my whatchamacallits." Instead, he said, "Tell me more about what you do and the challenges you face in trying to be successful at what you're doing."

By changing the questions, he could give his clients a fresh perspective on their business, often sharing some points of view, based on his experiences with other customers, that perhaps they had not thought of. It also allowed him to take an honest look at whether his products and services would have any value to his client. Sometimes that answer was no—there really was no added value. In which case he would tell them so, and he sometimes even offered one of his competitors as a solution to his client's problems.

Whoa . . . wait a minute. Did I just say that sometimes he would refer his prospective clients to his competition? Yes, that's exactly what he would do if he felt they could serve his clients better. Why? Because he realized one very important thing in business; collaboration will always lead to more success than simply competition. That's not to say that competition is bad. It's not. But if we only focus on competing instead of truly trying to help the people we serve, we're missing the point. No matter what our product or service may be, our goal should be to help people with that product or service. If our product or service cannot help them (or perhaps it's not the best way to help them), why wouldn't we try to find the best solution? Doing so accomplishes several things.

First, it's likely that the client will remember our integrity and our willingness to put their needs first. And in the future, when they come across someone who needs our products or services, they will refer them to us. Even our competitors may begin to act in a similar way. Both situations, however, are not the reason we want to change the focus from us to them. The primary reason is that doing the right thing is not only the right thing to do but also a profitable way to do business. Bob Burg says it best: "People generally do business with those they know, like, and trust."

In this new age of information, good news has become much easier to pass along, but bad news is even easier. It's more important than ever to have a good reputation and a good product or service.

But this is not a sales book; it's about how to achieve your goals, whether personal or in business. Changing the questions you're asking yourself—away from what your prospective clients or employees can do for you to what you can do for them—will ultimately come back to benefit you in ways you can't even imagine.

Now what about the day-to-day business stuff? How can the questions we ask help with the mundane, but necessary, day-to-day things we must do in our jobs? The report due at the end of the week? The time sheet we have to fill out today? The research we were asked to do for our supervisor? The shelves we have to stock before we can end our shift? The back-to-back double shift starting today? All those meetings we have to attend? No matter what our jobs are, we all have things to do that we are not excited about or tasks that don't have us jumping for joy as we start our days.

It's perhaps when we perform these tasks, more than any other, that we can most benefit from the questions we used to drive the conversations in our minds.

When we start with, "Why do I have to do such-and-such today?" because it's our least favorite part of our job, we have already begun a conversation that our computer brains will use to spit out answers—and begin the merry-go-round—that results in a painful, long, boring, and sometimes downright miserable day.

What if, instead, we began with, *"How could I completely reinvent the way I approach such-and-such a task today that will allow me to have fun while getting it done?"*

Or perhaps *"What kind of game could I turn such-and-such a task into that would make it fun for me and the people at work that also have to do it?"*

Or even *"If I had to come up with a way to make this task one that people at work wanted to do and started competing with each other to do, what could I come up with?"*

There are many questions you could ask to change your perspective. You might ask, "What's the point?" since you still have to accomplish the task and you know you hate doing it. Remember, this is not about getting out of doing your work, but how you can enjoy the process. Yes, you may still have to spend your day doing the task you dislike so much, but if you can change the way you think about it, a few things will happen.

First, you will immediately lower your stress by changing the way you look at the task. Second, with your new perspective, you may even find new ways of accomplishing the task that your old thinking prevented you from seeing. Third, you'll change your attitude at the beginning of the day and at the beginning of the task. These changes will ripple throughout the rest of your day and affect it positively. This can influence tomorrow and even the rest of your week—not to mention the days leading up to doing this task again later.

We should all constantly question what we do, how we are doing it, and why we do it in our careers, professions, and corporations. Not simply because the adage that we can always get better is true, but because this is not about constantly getting bigger and doing more. We should always question because the world is constantly changing. People are constantly changing and their needs change too. Whether they're our customers or our employees, we should always strive to change with them. By questioning where we are, what we are doing, and where we are going, we can continue to meet those needs.

The last thing I want to discuss, from a business perspective, pertains specifically to being a supervisor, manager, or executive. One of the most important things you can do in these roles is change the conversation you have in your mind (by asking different questions) regarding those who work for you.

Many in positions of authority are driven—usually with pressure from their boss or the board of directors—by the company's bottom line. Shareholders constantly want higher returns, and the stock market is a fickle mistress. Even not-for-profits must answer to their board of directors and the company budget.

This fiscal focus puts pressure on managers and executives to drive productivity by controlling their subordinates and micromanaging tasks because they are the supervisor/manager/executive for a reason, and they know best. This stems from the questions in their minds, which might sound like this: "How can I make sure we make our sales goal this month since my team is behind their projections?" or "How can we reduce our department budget by 10 percent and still get all our work done?" or even, "How can I get Sally to stop spending so much time on Facebook and more time on her job?"

You get the idea.

Here's the basic problem. Unless you own your own business, chances are, no matter how much you may like what you do, you're going to work to earn a paycheck. Sure, you want the company to succeed, but only from the perspective that as long as it succeeds, you keep getting paid. You're not likely to be concerned with all the things your boss is concerned with, mostly because you're not privy to all those things. If you're a supervisor or manager, you need to understand that your goals and those of your employees are not typically the same. What you focus on and what they focus on are not typically the same. Yep, you guessed it; you're both asking different questions.

So, how can you accomplish your goals if the questions you're asking (as they relate to your business goals) differ completely from the questions (and goals) of your subordinates?

The answer is you can't.

Am I saying that you need to get your subordinates to ask the same questions you do and start having the same goals? No. Actually, it's the other way around. You need to ask the same questions they do.

Hang on. Don't throw this book away just yet.

The point I'm trying to make is that as it relates to your employees, the best thing you can do is shift your focus away from what *you* want and put it squarely on what they want. Find out what their goals are as employees. Ask them what their ambitions are. Take a genuine interest in why they want to work at your company or in your department. Ask them regularly how they are doing in terms of enjoying their work.

Once you have a good understanding of why they are doing what they do and what they want to do in their careers, you'll be in a better position to understand how to help them be successful. That's right, your job as their supervisor is to help them be successful. Why? Because by doing so, you can ensure that the right people in your department are doing the right jobs in the best way possible.

But what if they're incompetent at their job or even miserable at it?

Let me ask you this. Do you want someone who is miserable at their job in your department? If they are horrible at it, is it because they are in the wrong job? Did they not get the proper training? Or do they hate what they do? All those situations are fixable, but you can't correct them if you're not aware they exist. If you find yourself in a situation where someone hates what they're doing, you need to help them move to another department or even another company so that you can find the right person for that job.

What does all of this do to help you with your own business goals? How can asking different questions about your employees, which focus on their wants and needs, help you achieve your own career wants and needs?

Everything.

One of the most predictable consequences of focusing on your employees and their happiness is that they will work harder (because they will enjoy their job) and be more productive, which will help you achieve the goals you need to achieve for the company.

In business, it's not always about the questions we ask regarding ourselves but—equally if not more important—the questions we ask concerning others, whether they are peers, employees, customers, vendors, or competitors.

Well, finally, here we are. We have delved into how questions play a role in our lives, both personally and in business. We have determined that those questions determine the self-talk or conversation that occurs constantly in our brains. We know that it's this conversation that then drives our thoughts—and those thoughts, which determine our focus, are the key to changing it all. What about the people we spend time with? If our goal is to be happy and our lives are impacted by the information we take in and those whom we associate with, shouldn't we examine how those questions play a role in our relationships?

Chapter 10
Relationships

Friends, lovers, partners, husbands, wives, and families; as human beings, we spend much of our lives searching for, working on, and maintaining our close relationships. Sometimes good, sometimes bad; we have all been there. They say that if you haven't been hurt; you have never really loved. I don't know if that's true, but I do know that almost everyone, at some point in their life, has been heartbroken, whether it's with a significant other, a best friend, or a family member. We have all had fights and said things we regret.

This chapter is not meant to be a guide to building the perfect relationship or having the perfect marriage—there are plenty of books on the totality of relationships. What I want to do is show you how the art of MOTIVESTIONS can play a role in this part of your life. By using questions, you can get more out of your relationships.

Remember that our goal in life is to be happy and to experience joy; this is probably the most important goal in our personal lives. There are a couple of sayings that always make me chuckle.

One is "A man is the king of his castle . . . until the queen moves in." The other is "If Mama ain't happy, ain't nobody happy."

How can we use the power of motivating questions to help us with our relationships and make sure that Mama is happy and that the king doesn't feel like he has lost control of his castle?

In the previous chapter, we touched on the skill of listening as a people skill, not just something that applies to businesspeople. Listening is perhaps the most significant ability you need in any relationship, and sadly, it's probably the one most people are the worst at. I believe open, honest, and frequent communication is the key to any good relationship. By open, honest, and frequent, I don't mean regularly scheduled yelling and screaming matches over who didn't do the dishes or take out the trash, or why the checkbook is missing three checks.

Learning to talk and listen to each other is perhaps the hardest, yet most important, thing you can do. It doesn't matter whether it's your spouse, partner, best friend, parent, or child. Have you ever heard, or better yet, said, any of the following statements?

- He never listens to me.
- She doesn't pay any attention to the things I say. Everything I say goes in one ear and out the other. I might as well be talking to the wall.
- What is the point of talking if you won't listen?

Sound familiar? Let me ask you this. If you've ever felt like or said any of those statements, then you know what it's like not to be heard? If you know how that makes you feel and how frustrating and unfair it is, why would you want to pass on those feelings to someone you care about?

Oh, I'm sure you're a much better listener than they are. I'm sure you never stop listening to what they're saying halfway through and start planning your own answer, or think about the points you want to make before they're done talking, right? You would never even consider being the type of person who can't wait for your conversation partner to shut up so you can tell them your story, which is so much better than the one they just told you, right?

Hopefully, you can read the sarcasm in my words.

I'm not saying you're a horrible person. It's part of being human that makes us act this way, but if we know how bad it makes us feel when someone isn't listening to us, then we need to learn how to control ourselves and become better listeners, so we don't make those we care about feel the same way. Does that make sense?

How do we do that? How can we become better listeners?

One way is to pay attention to that conversation in your head when conversing with someone. Learn to notice when you have stopped paying attention to what is being said, and when you're planning a response before they have finished talking. You can do this is by asking questions of yourself early on in the conversation:

> *How can I make sure they truly feel that I'm listening to every word they say?*
> *What can I do to make sure I hear everything they are telling me?*

What these questions can do is focus our attention on the speaker instead of our own desire to respond. You might answer the first question with something like "Make sure I'm looking them in the eye" or "Don't let my mind wander" or "Don't look down or around the room. Pay attention to them." You might answer the second question with, "Think about what they are saying, and then repeat back what I think I heard." You'll be focused on them and what they're saying, not on what you need to say next.

You will have plenty of time to get your story told later. Sometimes, the points we're trying to argue might get answered if we listen to what the other person is saying. By understanding their point of view, we can better position ourselves to know what they want or need and whether we can meet that need.

Too often, we feel that there shouldn't be any silence in our conversations. What's wrong with letting the other person fully express their thoughts and then taking a few moments to absorb what they just told us so we can plan a response? In this world of instant interaction and ease of electronic interchange, I think we've forgotten the art of communication.

If you were explaining something to someone and they listened intently to what you had to say, and then when you finished, they stood back, clearly thinking about what you just said before answering. Wouldn't that make you feel better? Wouldn't you feel they were giving considerable thought prior to answering you? If that makes you feel good, why not extend the same courtesy to others?

The best way to practice the art of conversation is to think about it before you talk and perhaps even during the conversation, until it becomes a force of habit you don't have to think about anymore. How, you ask? Why questions, of course!

Here are some questions you can ask before any conversation.

What is the purpose of this conversation?
What am I hoping to take away from this
  conversation?
What does this person want or need from me from this
  conversation?
How would I like this person to feel after our
  conversation?

What can I do to best serve both of us during our
conversation?
How can I remember to stay open-minded during the
conversation?
What can I do to stay engaged in this conversation?

You don't need to ask all of these before every conversation. Ask one or two to remind yourself that listening is not about you; it's about the person who is speaking. Stay focused on being a good listener so that when it's your turn to speak, you will have all the facts and information you need to make an informed, intelligent response. You'll find that your conversation is much more knowledgeable, and those you converse with are too.

Of course, every relationship has its difficulties, and, in every relationship, there are difficult discussions. Some people call them fights. There are also hard discussions over serious topics or just serious things that you both need to talk about. The first step is to remember that you love this person and that you truly care about them.

Whenever you're about to have a serious conversation or you become annoyed, frustrated, angry, or emotional with them, ask yourself:

How much does this person mean to me?

I know that's not always easy when your "sweet honey-bun" is being a colossal idiot. What's important, however, is to understand what you truly want. When you find yourself in the middle of, shall we say, a difference of opinion, try to answer one or both of the following questions:

What's more important, for us to understand each
other or for me to be right?
Would I rather resolve our differences and stop fighting,
or would I rather be right?

Sometimes that change of perspective is all we need. Yes, we all want to be right. We all want the other person to acknowledge that our perspective is the correct one, but when you think about it, how many times have you truly won the other person over? How many times have they said, "You know what, you're absolutely right. I have no idea what I was thinking, but your way is obviously better than mine"?

Do you know why this doesn't happen all that often? Because they are just as convinced that their perspective is the correct one as you are of yours.

Of course, sometimes a disagreement can involve a decision that has to be made and, in that case, you can't agree to disagree; a decision must be made. In those cases, it's important to understand that regardless of the outcome (whether you "win" or "lose" in the decision), you should also think about how you reach that outcome and how both of you will feel when you reach it.

You may want to ask yourself some questions before you get to the point where you either win or lose in the decision. Questions such as these:

> *Is there some way we can reach a decision where neither of us has to "lose"?*
> *If I don't "win" this disagreement, would it be the end of the world?*
> *What if I'm wrong and they are right? What would that point of view look like?*
> *How can I help them see that my way is the only way to go without them feeling as if I'm telling them they are wrong? (How can I help them look at my point of view through their own eyes?)*
> *What would our discussion sound like if we were both on the same side trying to solve this problem?*

Most of the time, however, you're more likely to have a difference of opinion or a disagreement. These types of discussions don't have to have a winner and a loser. No life-altering decisions need to be made; you simply disagree. How do you resolve these disagreements when you both want to be right and yet internally, you certainly don't want to "fight" with someone you care about? The first step is to pin down what's really going on with questions such as these:

> *How do I feel right now about this disagreement?*
> *(I.e., Are my feelings hurt? Do I feel like I'm not*
> *being listened to? Do I feel threatened by their point*
> *of view? And so on . . .)*

If you can better understand why you're disagreeing with them, you will find some resolution. The next step is to look at the reality of the disagreement by asking some of the following:

> *What is the worst thing that can happen if we don't*
> *solve this disagreement?*
> *What will happen to our relationship if they realize*
> *I'm right? What will happen to our relationship if I*
> *realize they are right?*

All that's left now is to get past the disagreement and to resolve the conflict in such a way that it doesn't harm your relationship. The best way to do so is to look outside of your own views and consider other possibilities. This doesn't mean you're wrong or that your point of view isn't correct. You may, in fact, ultimately arrive at the conclusion you were drawing, but the important thing is that you arrived there together rather than separately.

Here are some questions you can ask to cross the finish line together:

> *What would our conversation be like if neither of us*
> *had to be right?*

How would we approach this problem if we were working together to solve it for someone else? (I find that I'm usually much more open and honest when I'm trying to help others than I am when doing something for myself.)

What would I say if I wanted to better understand where they are coming from?

What if neither of our points of view are the best one? Is it possible there are other ideas we are not considering?

Am I willing to bet my next year's salary that I'm 100 percent right? (Sometimes we need to put our viewpoint into perspective in terms of how much we think it's worth.)

What would the answer be to our dilemma if we were told that the only way we could solve it would be to forget our respective ideas and to start over by finding a solution that we both could live with?

Since we are both passionate about our positions on this issue and we both care about the outcome, how could either of our ideas be "bad"?

What are the best parts of each of our ideas that might lead us to a new and better solution?

Although logic can drive many of our intellectual processes, it has very little to do with our emotional processing capabilities. Face it; we're probably at our most emotional when involved in an argument. Clearly, it's not a simple thing to think about—all these powerful perspective questions—when the subject is something we are passionate about.

Wouldn't it be great if there were a way to practice these relationship MOTIVESTIONS so that when we find ourselves challenged, they come to us as second nature? I see you nodding, and I hear you saying, "Why yes, yes it would." Well, guess what? There is.

Like almost everything, when it comes to learning a new skill, the most effective way to practice and harness that skill is to teach it. In this case, rather than starting your own MOTIVESTIONS training program, I'm talking about using the power of questions with your friends. This can be regarding relationship issues, personal issues, business issues, or . . . well, you get the idea. When a friend comes to you for advice, try to resist the urge to tell them what you think or, heaven forbid, tell them what to do. Instead, use questions to help them reach the answers themselves.

Use your newfound skill of MOTIVESTIONS to help them see things from a different perspective, to look at alternative points of view, or to challenge their beliefs and habits. These skills will help them find new ways to view their challenges and, ultimately, to find solutions that help them move toward their goals.

Through practicing your questions by helping your friends, you'll accomplish two things. First, when it comes to others, you're less likely to be emotionally charged about their situations. This allows you to look objectively, honestly, and with a clear head, and that will lead you to generate more motivating questions to help them find better solutions. The second benefit is that you'll be helping your friend, family member, or significant other by helping them see outside of their own emotionally charged thinking, and they will envisage new possibilities they previously could not see.

This all leads to the final component in your journey to success through MOTIVESTIONS: the Invisible Ink of Giving.

Chapter 11
Giving: The Invisible Ink

I thought I had it all figured out. After years of reading, rereading, listening, talking, and studying, I felt I had dissected the DNA of Success and found the core that answered my burning questions about why people do what they do and what makes some more successful than others.

It was simple enough that I could teach it to anyone just starting out, and yet comprehensive enough to help even the most ardent student of personal achievement. After I figured out the "feeling" component that had been missing from my research, I thought to myself, "Eureka!" It all made sense and it all fit together. It was as though I had completed a jigsaw puzzle, then stood back, and marveled at how beautiful the picture looked.

When I was a child, I loved learning how to write in "invisible ink," which usually involved lemon juice or some other secret spy-type way to hide messages. As I began writing this book, I was introduced to something I hadn't yet seen in my studies. This concept was something that, looking back, was an undercurrent or theme for some of the research I had done, but hadn't stood out to me specifically. It was the invisible ink of the books, lectures, and seminars in my study of human nature over the years.

That concept—which now seems so simple to me but had eluded me in my study over the years—is the concept of giving to or helping other people. No need to scratch your head. I never said it was something earth shattering (though it really is) or some newly discovered panacea to success (though it really is).

Helping other people—giving of ourselves, instead of wanting only to get from others—is the truest secret of success I know. It will help you in any and every area of your life: in business, in personal relationships, and in your financial, spiritual, emotional, and physical life. Nothing will help you more than focusing on helping other people instead of focusing on yourself.

Perhaps the most concrete example of how giving can help you is found in the Go-Giver books by Bob Burg and John David Mann. The parables in The Go-Giver and It's Not About You are phenomenal in helping drive home the point that if we can take the focus off ourselves and put it on helping others, we'll inevitably achieve more than we ever could had we set out to only help ourselves.

Although Bob and John's books are geared toward business, their principles apply to every area of our lives.

What does giving have to do with MOTIVESTIONS, you ask? It's the invisible ink that changes your questions from simple inquiries to powerful motivating forces that will propel your life and your life experience to levels you never imagined.

The key is to get into the habit of asking questions whose answers will benefit other people. The best definition of success I heard went something like this: "To do what I want, whenever I want, with whomever I want and, whenever possible, to help others in the process."

In some ways, this might seem simple to you, and in others, it may seem impossible. In almost every instance, there is always a way to consider it in terms of helping others. Let's look at some examples.

Remember the questions we talked about in terms of dieting? Instead of simply asking, *"How can I lose weight for good and enjoy the process?"* try asking this instead:

> *How can I lose weight for good and enjoy the process?*
> *Who could I share this with to help them as well?*

What about personal questions that deal with challenges we face? Does the idea of focusing on giving work there too? Let's take a look.

Remember trying to overcome fear? We talked about asking, *"When in my life have I felt powerful? How can I channel that feeling right now?"*

Try adding this to your question:

> *Who do I know that would benefit from being able to channel this feeling of power?*
> *How can I make sure that I pay attention to how I do this so that I can help that person later?*

Did you notice the trick I put into this one? Not only are you asking about how you can help someone, but also about how to teach them, which means you must focus on how you're doing something so you can better show them the process. This will also take your mind off the fear and focus it on learning to teach your friend. Tricky, huh?

Remember this one? *"How can I have fun asking her out regardless of her answer?"*

With just a little tweaking, we can change the focus:

> *How can I have fun asking her out regardless of her answer, and how can I make sure she doesn't feel uncomfortable in the process?*

Now, you might think, "OK, I can see how some of these are easy to change, but what about the questions that only apply to me?" Maybe something like *"What am I happy about in my life right now?"*

Of course, you could ask a different question instead of assuming that it's impossible. Something like:

> *What if I wanted to help others when asking this question? What would that look like?*

Sorry, I couldn't resist.

Here is one way to change the perspective:

> *What am I happy about in my life right now, and how can I use this focus to help brighten someone else's day?*

Instead of simply asking, *"What areas of study really interest me?"* try *"What areas of study really interest me and who do I know that might also be interested and might make it fun for both of us to study together?"*

Certainly, there are times when the conversation in your mind is about you and only you. I'm not saying that you need to focus on helping other people with every question you ask yourself. However, if, whenever possible, you try to ask questions that will not only help you but will also help others, you'll find that your life improves dramatically in every area. You'll start to impact the lives of others, and you'll begin to, as Gandhi so eloquently put it, "Be the change you wish to see in the world."

Will this help you become more successful? Absolutely, but that's not why you should do it.

Will this make your life more fulfilling? Yes, but remember, this isn't only about you.

Will this help you achieve your own goals and dreams faster? Yep. This is one of those laws of life you simply can't avoid, which states that if you focus on helping others, help will come back to you—not always in the way you might think, but also in increasing proportion to the amount of effort you put into helping others and the number of people you help.

Up to this point, we have talked about what the concept of MOTIVESTIONS is. We have discussed how it works, what it does, and how you can apply it to your life. The only thing left to do is to help you get started. It's time to learn how to build your MOTIVESTIONS muscle.

Chapter 12
Improving Your IQ

Like everything else in life that's new to us, it takes time to build the muscles we need to be good at asking questions. In this case, we're talking about the muscle of your mind. Face it. You've been asking questions since the day you were born, processing information, trying to determine what it meant to you and how it applied to your life. The way you've been asking those questions, however, has mostly been reactive, not proactive.

Your brain's neurons have been firing this way ever since they were formed. These are some seriously ingrained habits we are talking about, and they aren't going to change overnight simply because you're reading this book. In fact, unlike learning a new sport or trying some new routine, you don't have the luxury of starting a new path. You must train your brain to think differently as it deals with the inputs of daily life by asking questions all day, every day, the way it has always done. I mean, it's not as if you can simply stop asking questions in those thousands of thoughts you have each day while you change the habit.

We must figure out how to change the way you run while you are running. Sounds crazy I know, but don't worry, you can do it.

You must figure out a way to show your incredible mind that there is a new and better way to be. Rather than adding to those thoughts every day, let's begin by simply changing a few of them.

This is what I call changing your IQ—meaning, of course, your intentional questioning.

Remember when we talked about the questions that automatically kick in the minute you wake up in the morning? Those autopilot questions you use to start your day? Well, some of them are necessary—the "Should I hit snooze or get up?" and "Should I wake the kids or get in the shower first?" types of questions. What happens is that interspersed with the "What should I eat for breakfast?" and "When do I have to leave to get to work on time?" questions are the reactive ones that deal with things you're worried about.

Questions like these: "What do I have to do today?" "Did I finish all my homework?" "How can I get out of having to go to work/school today?" "Why can't I just stay in bed?"

Improving your intentional questioning (IQ) will change your focus from answering autopilot questions to asking motivating questions you control. To begin, ask general questions. Remember that we're working a new muscle, so don't do too much on day one.

General questions are ones that help you focus on positive aspects of your day. It may not be what you focus on that's important as much as the fact that you direct the focus. Here are a few examples of brilliant Morning IQ questions you can ask:

How can I start my day today expecting to succeed?
What am I happy about in my life now?
What am I excited about in my life now?
What amazing adventure will I have today?

The best way to improve your IQ is to write down a list of questions you want to ask yourself in the morning. It's not enough to simply think of the questions and hope that you remember them. Your brain will already try to focus on the autopilot questions and the other reactive questions that want to creep into your conscious thinking the moment you wake up. By writing the questions down, you're signaling to your brain that this is important. You'll be forcing it to focus on the questions long enough to write them down, which reinforces the original thoughts you had when you came up with them and now you have something to refer to in the morning.

Put the list by your bed, right next to, in front of, or even on top of your alarm clock. Whatever it takes to remind you where the questions are and that now is the time to think about them. Once you wake up, try to form the habit of asking your Morning IQ questions immediately.

You won't have to ask every question every day. Even one or two questions on your list will make a tremendous impact on how your brain processes and on your outlook for that day. This will shift those neurons in your brain into realizing that there are new and better questions you can ask, and by being intentional in your morning questioning, you can affect the rest of your day positively.

The second step to building this muscle is to change your IQ in the evening.

Right now, if you're like I used to be, you most likely go to bed exhausted after a long day. And although your head hits the pillow and you barely have enough energy to turn out the light, your brain isn't finished. When I used to close my eyes—looking forward to that peaceful night's sleep—my mind would suddenly find itself some free time. It was no longer dealing with all the autopilot questions of "What should I eat for dinner?" and "Should I go to bed or finish that report first?" or "Can I get away without brushing my teeth tonight?" Now I could focus on all the other things that were swimming around in my mind. As soon as my eyelids shut, my brain would turn on and flash questions across my mind's eye:

"What did I forget to do today?"

"What did I do that left me so tired today?"

"How can I deal with that problem at work that happened today?"

"Why is so-and-so mad at me? What did I do?"

And on and on they would go until pure exhaustion kicked in and I finally fell asleep.

Of course, even when my conscious mind is asleep, my subconscious is still wide awake. Whatever I'm thinking about as I fall asleep is what's going to be tackled first because it's my subconscious's job to process the things my conscious mind didn't have time to deal with. Go to sleep thinking about all the problems you had today, and that's what you'll be thinking about all night long.

How about we change that conversation? Here are some great general Evening IQ questions you can ask:

> *What are all the good things that happened to me today?*
> *What are all the things I accomplished throughout my day today?*
> *What am I most grateful for today?*
> *What am I most proud of doing today?*
> *What was the most enjoyable thing I did today?*

The trick with Evening IQ questions is that they should be the last thing you think about at night. If you like to read before bed, go ahead. Read first, and then ask your questions right after you turn that light off. If you have a significant other that wants to chat in the dark before you fall asleep, fine, chat away; then ask your questions before you drift off.

Remember, you don't have to ask dozens of questions; one or two will do. The key is to focus on the answers and how they feel. Just like the morning questions, make a list. Write down as many questions as you can come up with and put the list by your bed. Don't put it in the bathroom or in your closet unless you plan on sleeping there. This needs to be the last thing you focus on; not the next to last or third from last, but the last thing.

To fully ingrain this habit, work on your Morning and Evening IQ for twenty-eight days or four weeks. Every morning, wake up and start your day by asking some MOTIVES-TIONS IQ questions. Intentional questions are simply one type of MOTIVESTIONS that can help integrate this process into your life. You can focus on the answers as you go about your morning ritual, but make sure you ask the questions before you get out of bed, so your brain knows it has a task to do by answering them. Think of as many answers as you can while you brush your teeth, take a shower, get dressed, put on makeup—and remember to concentrate on how those answers make you feel.

At night, right before you fall asleep, reach over, and just before you turn off that light, review your list of evening questions and pick out a couple you can focus on. Close your eyes, relax, ask the questions, and then answer them, with as many answers as you can come up with.

You don't have to use the same list of questions for twenty-eight days; you can change them around. Add new ones and delete old ones—it's up to you. There's no right or wrong way to do this. The only criteria are that the questions need to be motivating, either generally or specifically, regarding your goals. After you've done this for two weeks, change one of your questions to be more specific about a goal that you want to achieve. In the morning, you might ask:

> *What is one step that I can take toward my goal of (fill in the blank) today?*

*How can I make sure that I have an exciting day
today and move toward my long-term goal?*

In the evening you can also be more specific:

*What are all the ways I made progress towards my
goal today?*
*How does my successful step toward my goal today
make it easier for me to get even closer in the near
future?*

What happens at the end of twenty-eight days? I'm glad you asked.

If you follow through and increase your intentional questioning every morning and every evening, by the end of the twenty-eighth day, you won't even have to think about it. This will be something you do every day for the rest of your life, and you'll be amazed at how powerful an impact it will have on your life and the lives of those around you.

You can, of course, decide that twenty-eight days of awesomesauce is enough for you and make a conscious effort to stop. You can go back to the autopilot and reactive questions of your past, because living a life of passion and intended joy is not for you. The choice is entirely yours.

Here is the exciting part. Once this idea of asking empowering, motivating questions every morning and every evening takes hold, your brain will have evidence it can draw on for implementing MOTIVESTIONS in the rest of your day.

Now that you know that asking the right questions can have a positive, powerful impact on your life, the only remaining step is to pay attention to the rest of your day. This goes back to those feelings, to learning how to notice your physiology. Anytime you feel down, sad, or miserable, any feeling that's not a joyful, happy feeling that you know you want to feel, you only have to do one thing: pull out the Power of Why!

Ask yourself why you feel that way. What conversation

is taking place in your mind that's making you feel such a negative emotion? Once you have identified that emotion, simply look at the questions you're asking yourself that drive that conversation. All you have to do now is change the questions to change the way you feel.

Remember that when you're feeling joyful and having an amazing day, you don't need to do anything; you're already asking the right MOTIVESTIONS. If you're feeling neutral, neither happy nor sad, you can choose whether you want to focus on your inner conversation and questions. You're the one in charge. By paying attention to your feelings, you'll know when you need to change the conversation and improve your IQ.

It all starts with the twenty-eight days of practice. After a while, asking intentional questions become as normal as breathing, and you'll notice in every area of your life that your outlook and your outcomes are improving. Of course, you also have the option of continuing your twenty-eight-day IQ questions. You can start over with even more specific ones, or you can ask detailed questions about new short-term or long-term goals you want to work toward. By coming up with intentional questions that you ask every morning and evening, you'll be focusing the power of that incredible mind of yours into focusing and taking action toward those goals.

Now that you know how it works, here are some tools to start out with so you can start changing your life right now!

Chapter 13
The motivestions Toolbox

You should have a pretty good understanding of the MOTIVESTIONS framework by now. To change the conversation in your head, you need to take charge of the questions you're asking. This will determine the consistent thoughts you have, and it will set your focus, which, in turn, will drive the actions you take. Ultimately, it's those actions that will move you either closer to or further away from any goal you set. It doesn't matter if it's a large long-term goal or a tiny "in the next hour" goal. The whole point is to enjoy the journey of life, which is to find joy and happiness in everything you do.

To make MOTIVESTIONS work, you need to practice this new skill. Like all habits, improving your IQ is simply a matter of practice.

Here are some suggested Morning IQ questions to help you:

MORNING IQ

How can I start my day today expecting to succeed?
What am I happy about in my life now?
What am I excited about in my life now?
What am I excited about that's going to happen today?
Who am I looking forward to seeing today?
What am I proud of in my life?
What am I grateful for in my life?
What am I enjoying most in my life right now?
What am I committed to in my life now?
What am I looking forward to right now?
Yesterday was awesome; what else is possible today?
What can I do to remember to smile at everyone I meet today?
Who do I love?
Who loves me?
Who cares about me?
What are some examples of things that I have done in the past that I can draw from to help overcome the challenges I have today?
How can I make my own luck today?
What amazing adventure will I have today?
Whose life am I going to brighten today? (Sometimes taking your eyes off yourself and putting them on others can help you overcome your own challenges.)
What memories am I going to make today?

MORNING IQ NOTES:

Remember, you only need to begin by asking two or three questions each morning. It's important to ask these questions as soon as you wake up. Having a list near your bed so that you see it first thing is the best way to remind yourself to do this until it becomes a habit.

These are just a few example questions; you should make your own list that resonates with you. Choose some from this list and add your own, or simply start anew and create your personal Morning IQ list.

When answering the questions, try to come up with as many answers as you can during your morning routine. Also, don't just think of the answers; think about how they make you feel. Try to feel the emotion your answers elicit from you. The more you learn to feel while you build your IQ muscles, the more powerful your results will be.

The end of your day is also an important time to practice your new skill. Learning to change your mind's natural habit of recounting all the struggles you encountered that day and listing all the worries and unfinished work you have to do will make a significant and immediate impact on your life.

During the next twenty-eight days, when you start using your Morning IQ list, create a separate list of Evening IQ questions. Although some questions may appear on both morning and evening lists, the purpose of the evening list is to reflect on all the positive events and accomplishments of your day.

Here are some suggested Evening IQ questions:

EVENING IQ

What are all the good things that happened to me today?
What are all the things I accomplished today?
What am I most grateful for today?
What am I most proud of doing today?
What was the most enjoyable thing I did today?
What was the best thing that happened to me today?
Who smiled at me today?
What made me smile or laugh today?
What was the most unexpected surprise today?
What am I looking forward to most tomorrow?

Who loves me?

Who do I love?

*What is one thing did I do today that was nice for
someone else? Now another . . . and another . . .*

How much more exciting can tomorrow be?

*What one thing did I do to move toward a goal I
have, large or small, long term or short?*

What challenge(s) did I overcome today?

What was my best feeling of the day today?

What was amusing about my day today?

EVENING IQ NOTES:

As with the morning questions, you only need to begin
by asking two or three questions each evening. The key is
to ask these questions right before you fall asleep. Ideally,
you want to look at your list of questions as you get ready to
turn out the light. Choose a couple of questions to focus on,
then lay back, close your eyes, and ask them. This way, the
last thing your conscious mind focuses on before you rest is
answering these powerful intentional questions.

Once again, these are just example questions. You should
make your own list that resonates with you.

Although this can be challenging when falling asleep,
try to come up with as many answers as you can, and most
importantly, think about how those answers make you feel.

By using the Morning and Evening IQ exercises for
twenty-eight days, you'll be retraining your mind to focus
on things you choose to focus on. This will begin building
the muscle you can use to elicit MOTIVESTIONS whenever
you choose.

The Morning and Evening IQ question lists I suggest
are purposefully general in nature. As you practice this new
skill, you can use questions that are both general enough to
answer and that will change the negative mindset that most
of us have developed over the course of our lives.

Once you get the hang of it, add more specific questions to your list—questions that are targeted toward your specific goals and dreams, large and small. I would suggest, however, that you don't only use specific questions in your Morning and Evening IQ exercises. Try to always ask at least one general question and then add one or two specific questions. This way, you're not only focusing on the "work" of your goals and dreams, but also on the general happiness and joy in your life. Remember, this is about enjoying the journey along the way, not just the destination.

As you add goal- and dream-specific questions, remember to keep them positive. Don't simply ask, *"What two things can I do to further my business today?"*

Try to get creative. *"What two things can I do to further my business today and be totally excited about doing?"* Or *"How can I turn the two next steps in furthering my business into exciting adventures today?"*

And don't forget, whenever possible, to incorporate helping others into your questions. There are a lot of emotions we might feel on any given day; we may want to use our intentional questions to get back on track toward the life we want to have. Here are some suggested questions for some of those feelings. Questions you can have in the back of your mind so that anytime you're feeling one of these emotions, you have some ideas about how to change that conversation.

Depressed/Down/Blue

What is the one thing, right now, that I can think about that will make me smile?

What memory do I have in my past that was a time when I was passionate and excited?

What would my answer be if I was told that I would not receive any more in my life unless I could list ten things that I'm grateful for now?

If I could focus on only one thing that makes me happy for the next hour, what would I choose?

Overwhelmed/Stressed

What is one step that I could take right now to begin moving and stop feeling overwhelmed?

What is the most important thing on my list to do, and what is one thing that I can do to accomplish it? If not that, what is the next most important one?

If I wasn't worrying about this, what can I think of in my life that I would be happy about?

If I didn't have these stresses in my life, what would be the most important thing to me?

What is a goal worthy of my time that completely excites me?

What is one thing I could do right now to help ease the stress/worry that I'm feeling?

Angry

What is one point of view that's actually funny about this situation?

What would it take for me to let go of my charged emotion and not let this bother me, apart from getting my way?

What is the most important thing in my life right now? Is this issue worth keeping me from focusing on what means the most to me?

Will this situation matter tomorrow? Next week? Next month? Next year? Should I lend any more of my time to it now if it will not matter later?

What is the funniest movie I ever saw? What was the funniest scene in that movie?

If I didn't want to be angry right now, what would I do?

If I wanted to let this anger fall off my back, how would I think about the situation differently?

If I were advising my child or best friend about how to get past this anger, what advice would I give them?

When have I faced a situation where I was furious but could get beyond it quickly? How did I do that?

Frustrated/Annoyed
Start with

Why am I frustrated/annoyed?

What conversation in my head is making me feel this way?

How can I refocus my questions to change the conversation?

Then ask

Who do I know that never seems to get frustrated/ annoyed? How would they handle this situation?

When I think about what is frustrating/annoying me right now, how can I look at things differently that would make things humorous instead of annoying?

I have twenty-four hours in my day today. Which hours have been amazingly positive that I can focus on instead of this one?

Whoever is frustrating me may not be aware that I'm frustrated. How can I see things from another perspective to help move past all this?

When have I ever caused someone else to be frustrated? How did we resolve it then and how can that help me now?

If I knew there was a solution to getting past this frustration and that by finding it, I would earn a reward, how would I find that solution?

Lonely
Start with

What specifically is making me feel lonely right now? (Or Why am I feeling lonely right now?)

What questions am I asking/answering that make me feel this way?

How can I reframe the questions in such a way that it would stop making me feel like this?

Then ask

Who are all the people who care about and love me?

Who are all the people I care about and love?

Who do I enjoy spending time with that I can get together with while I work on finding someone?

What can I do to improve myself or become the type of person who the person I want to attract would want to meet?

What are some things I like to do? How can I find clubs/leagues related to these activities so that I might meet people with similar interests?

What are two hobbies that I have always wanted to try or new skills I have wanted to learn, and how can I fill some of my free time with them?

How can I keep myself busy so I don't have time to feel this way as I work toward my goal of becoming the person I want to be?

How can I learn to be OK with being alone without giving up my desire to be with someone or settling for never finding someone?

Being Apart

What are three ways that I can come up with to communicate with the person I'm missing?

What is something artistic and/or creative that I could do to show them how much I miss them?

Is there an event or special occasion I could plan for when I'm going to see them again that I could surprise them with?

What is the funniest memory we have made together? How can I recreate that feeling inside of me right now?

What are some things this person does that make me
feel loved? How can I focus on those things right
now and remember how they made me feel?

Frightened/Anxious
Start with

Why am I feeling frightened/anxious right now
specifically?
What am I saying to myself to make me feel this way?
What questions should I be asking instead that would
keep me from feeling this way?
What questions could I be asking to make me feel
powerful, strong, empowered, and confident?

Then ask

When have I faced a situation in my life that
prompted uncertainty or fear that I was able to
overcome? How did I do that? How can I apply that
knowledge to this situation?
What makes me feel empowered and powerful?
What would my friends say if they asked to list my
"incredible" traits?
How often in my life have things turned out better
than I thought they would?
When do I feel the most secure/safe? Why did I feel that
way? How can I feel that way now?
How will I feel when things turn out the way I want
them to in this situation?
Who could I talk to right now to help me calm down?
What would I say to help someone else if they were
feeling this way?
How likely is it that my fears will never actually
materialize based on my experiences?
How have I overcome fear/anxiety in the past?

Inadequacy/Low Self-Esteem

Who do I know that I think is very confident? How can I emulate them now?

When in my life have I felt the most confident? What made me feel that way?

What are three examples of times in my past when I was amazing?

What are five things I love about myself?

What would I do/say to help my best friend who was feeling this way?

How can I get better at the skill or ability that is making me feel this way? What one action can I take right now toward that?

What are some things I used to struggle with that I'm great at now? How did I do that? How can I take similar action in this situation?

What is more important, the way others think of me or the way I think of myself?

Negativity/Self Doubt

What is one positive about this situation? What is another one?

How can I look at this if I'm not allowed to think negatively about it?

How will I feel if the outcome I really want actually happens?

How many times in my life have things turned out right instead of the way I was worried they would?

Who are the most positive people I know? How would they look at this?

What would I say to my child if they were feeling this way?

What could I do right now to change the way I feel if my life depended on doing so?

Is it possible that I'm not thinking about how capable I am in this situation?

Is it possible that there is another viewpoint to this?

What if I really can change the way I'm thinking about this, and by doing so, I can change the outcome? How great would that be?

What if just because something happened in the past doesn't mean it will happen this time?

What is another instance in my history where the past didn't equal the future?

Failure

What can I learn from this? And if there is something I can learn, then have I really failed?

Who do I know (or have heard/read about) that has failed, only to bounce back and be even more successful than they originally intended or aimed for?

What is my definition of failure in this instance? Is that definition serving me?

Have I completely given up or is this just a setback?

What are some positive outcomes from this?

How can I use this experience to help others who are going through similar situations now or might face them in the future?

Using the adage "It's not how far you fall, but how quickly you bounce back up," what is one thing I can do now to help myself bounce back?

What is the opportunity disguised as an impossible situation here? How can I use this as a stepping stone to something better?

Looking back, what are some of the incredible positives I have experienced since the time I started until now?

Disappointment

Is this simply a detour on my road to my goal?

What is my measure of achievement for this situation?

What are some smaller components that perhaps I didn't realize I have achieved?

*How can I look at this and recognize the positive
impact it has had on my life?*

*What do I need to pay attention to in this instance
about how it feels so that I can help someone else in
the future who goes through a similar feeling?*

*When is an instance in my past where I experienced
disappointment and overcame it? How did I do
that?*

*Am I disappointed in myself or in the situation? What
can I do to prevent this from happening in the
future?*

*What can I do today to help move me past this and
begin my next achievement goal?*

Who do I know that can help me move past this?

*What are some areas of life that I'm doing really well
with right now, and how can I channel those wins
into this disappointing area of my life?*

Emergency Questions

There are many emotions you might feel at any given
moment on any given day. And although this toolbox may
not have listed them all, there is one more tool I want to
give you. It's what I call the "ER IQs" or simply Emergency
Questions. These are for those moments when maybe you
have a multitude of emotions running through you, or life
is throwing a rapid machine gun of "life happens" events at
you, and although they're not debilitating or major events,
they can be overwhelming.

You want to overcome them, but you can't figure out
what category they fit into because they're coming at you
so fast. That's where this ER IQ list can help.

What is beautiful around me right now?

What, in this moment, is good?

*What are the most important people/things in my life
at this moment?*

Who loves me?

Who do I love?

What is something that makes me smile?

What is something that always makes me laugh?

What are all the things that I'm grateful for in my life right now?

What is something right here, right now, in my immediate vicinity that I'm grateful for?

Which of the following do I possess? Good health, a roof over my head, food to eat, loving family members, freedom, friends?

Who is someone I'm close to that I could call for advice or a friendly ear?

What are my dreams, and what are the things about my dreams that excite me the most?

How does it get better than this? What else is possible?

If I stepped back from the situation and only focused on the things in my life that truly matter, how would that feel?

AFFIRMATIONS

Finally, here are example affirmations. Like IQs, these are intentional ways to change the conversation in your brain. Rather than questions, however, they're statements you can repeat, like a mantra, to help your brain drown out some of the negative feelings or input you might be receiving.

Use affirmations to help as a maintenance tool once you're out of the Pit of Despair or before you fall into it. There may be times when you're not down in the Pit of Despair, but you still feel negative enough that questions by themselves aren't working. Affirmations are a great way to help bring a turnaround in your mindset and get you back to where your questions are working for you once again. Affirmations are simply a self-talk tool to help you stay focused on all the good in your life.

I'm safe and I'm loved.

I expect good things to happen, and I deserve them.

I'm strong and brave and I have everything I need to be successful.

I'm kind and caring and those who know me don't judge me.

I'm a giving and loving individual and good things are coming my way.

I'm grateful for all that I have, and all I have is all I need.

I can overcome any challenges I may meet.

I'm focused on my goal and it's coming closer every day. Life is an adventure and I'm excited about living mine.

Prosperity and financial freedom are drawn to me.

Peace of mind and security are part of my life.

I'm healthy and full of life. Today is going to be a glorious day.

My business (career) is thriving, and I'm helping more and more people every day.

I have all the skills and tools necessary to be the best I can be.

Everything that happens in my life is happening for my ultimate good.

I forgive myself for mistakes that I made in the past. I look toward the future fearlessly and I'm present in the gift of today.

I love and approve of myself just the way I am.

I trust myself and trust that my decisions are the decisions I'm supposed to make.

I matter in the world, and what I have to offer, no one else can offer the same way.

Wonderful things are headed my way.

Kindness is drawn to me, just as I'm kind to others.

I surround myself with people who care about me, and more people who care are coming my way.

I'm beautiful and intelligent and people see me for all that I am.

I don't settle for less than what I deserve. I am drawn to things that are best for me.

I trust in my abilities, and fear doesn't have any hold over me.

Everything will work out for my highest good and the good of others.

I seek new ways to look at any situation that's holding me back.

I'm happy in my own skin and in my life experiences.

I'm more than good enough and getting better every day.

Every day, in every way, I'm getting stronger, better, and more able to handle the challenges that life sends my way.

I have more than enough.

All that I need will come to me when the time is right.

I attract only happiness in my life.

Money flows into my life easily, and I am and always will be financially secure.

I act and believe in such a way that success is drawn to me.

I attract only caring and kind people into my life.

Chapter 14
Real Life

Well, here we are. You have made it this far and you're still with me. We've covered a lot of information, and you're probably a little overwhelmed at the thought of it all. I mean, how is all of this supposed to work, really? It sounds good conceptually, but how does it apply in real life?

That's the ultimate question, isn't it?

I started this book with the goal of teaching you how to use MOTIVESTIONS in your life immediately, a tool you can use every day and one you can apply to your long-term goals—whatever they may be.

One more reminder before we wrap things up. The concept of MOTIVESTIONS is not a cure-all or silver bullet meant to be the answer to all that ails you. This is a tool to help you improve your life daily. Although I believe it can make an immeasurable difference in your life and vastly improve how you live day to day, it's not meant as a substitution for any medical care you might need due to diagnosed mental or physical health concerns. The brain is an incredibly complex organ, and science is only beginning to understand the various ways we can treat those with brains that function differently. Clinical depression, anxiety, or other mental health concerns should be treated like any other medical condition, and you should seek a medical professional to help you.

MOTIVESTIONS can serve as a tool, but there are myriad advances in the mental health field and medication-assisted therapy that you should consider. Now then, let's put everything together one last time to make sure you can start using this skill effectively, immediately, and start living your life to the fullest.

It all begins with your feelings, both emotional and physical. Life is meant to be lived, not simply endured as a series of frustrations and miserable experiences. Don't get me wrong; it's good to have challenges. It may not always seem like it, but those challenges make life worth living. It would be boring if everything went the way we wanted it to all the time, every day, all day long.

Most of us don't pay attention to how we respond to those challenges. Our emotions in those moments are the key. Noticing how you're feeling at any given moment is where this all begins. Again, I'm not suggesting you spend every waking moment asking yourself, "How am I feeling?" Most of the time, you're likely feeling fine. Life goes on. You're doing the things you need to do or want to do that day, and your experience of life may be quite pleasant.

But it's important to focus when we notice we don't feel well emotionally—those moments when life challenges us and our response has us feeling down, angry, frustrated, or in any way *not* experiencing that feeling of joy and happiness we truly crave. Being able to notice the difference in these feelings from those you normally experience is the first step to changing your life. It takes some practice, but now that you realize your brain is always asking questions, directing those questions intentionally, and understanding why you're feeling unhappy should not be difficult. It will become easier with time and practice.

Once you've identified when you're feeling unhappy or when your experience of life is not bringing you the joy you would like, you can challenge that conversation in your head. This is when you can take control of the questions and begin asking intentional questions that will serve you, instead of simply reacting to your environment on autopilot. Become a detective of your own story—the story of your life. Find out why you're feeling the way you are. Ask the right questions to help you understand what makes you feel this way. Once you know *why* something is happening in your life, you can quickly change the questions to change the way you feel.

I know it sounds simple, and it is. It's just not easy at first, but it will become easier as you practice.

Don't expect miraculous transformations. You're not likely to wake up tomorrow bounding out of bed and tackling new adventures in your life with no challenges or negative emotions to stop you. This is real life we're talking about, not a movie.

What will happen, though, is that you will notice a shift in the way you think. The way you tackle challenges, large or small, will begin to change. You'll become more accepting and less anxious about small things, and the larger challenges will seem less daunting and more manageable.

It's worth repeating here that life-changing events, those really heavy challenges that are a part of our lives, cannot and should not be expected to simply roll off your shoulders by using your newly acquired MOTIVESTIONS skills. We all need to process those large events in our lives. Part of who we are is a result of the major challenges we have faced throughout our lives. Trying to shortchange that process of absorbing, processing, and perhaps learning from those challenges would interfere with making you the person you are. You need to be able to do that. Give yourself time;

focus on what you need to do for yourself, and perhaps others, during those occasions in your life. When the time is right—you'll know when that is—you can turn to your new skills to help you get back to that state of happiness and joy you're meant to have. Use the Power of If when you need to, and before you know it, you'll be back to living your life at the full speed of happiness.

Remember that changing your feelings by asking the proper intentional questions will not always be easy. You might know intellectually that you want to change, and you might even understand what you need to do to change, but you still may not be able to get yourself to take the action of changing those questions to do it. Emotions are powerful, and when they're negative, they can have a powerful hold over our ability to act. There are two simple MOTIVESTIONS rules that can help you.

If you don't like the way you feel, ask a different question. Keep asking different questions until you change the way you feel.

If you can't bring yourself to start asking different questions to change the way you feel, you need to change the way you're feeling by changing your physiology. Changing your physical state by moving, talking, or acting differently or by breathing will change your state of feeling, which will then enable you to begin asking the right questions to change the way you feel.

Start with the Morning and Evening IQ questions. Write down your own question list and keep updating it as your goals and experiences change. Develop the muscle slowly, consistently, every morning and every evening, until taking control of questions becomes something you do automatically. Then, as your day-to-day life goes on, focus on those unhappy feelings, and try out various questions to see how they change your feelings and affect your life. Adjust and adapt your questions as you go.

I know it sounds simple, and I have already told you it's not easy. Now I have one last question for you.

What if I'm right?

What if taking charge of the questions you ask yourself can truly make an impact in your life? What if the small, day-to-day changes this practice has on your life will improve other areas of your life? Maybe you begin to enjoy your job more or it starts to positively affect your relationship. Maybe you begin to see opportunities and possibilities you never saw before simply because of these changes. What if removing the smaller challenges that used to derail your goals now frees you up to focus and pursue them more successfully?

Remember back in grade school? I don't know about you, but when we were kids, my friends and I would often "dare" each other to do things we were afraid of or unsure of. If it was something important, one of us would say to the other, "I double-dog dare you to do it."

I'm not sure I ever learned what a "double-dog dare" was or why it was more important than a simple dare, but I knew that if you didn't do something that someone double-dog dared you to do, you were considered the biggest chicken on the planet.

Here's where this gets interesting. What if, a year from now, you look back and realize your life has changed dramatically? What if just changing the way you approach your life ultimately begins to change the lives of the people in your sphere of influence? What if just by your actions, you begin to affect other people's actions as well? What if you begin to achieve your dreams, not just the day-to-day ones, but the large ones as well? And what if, by achieving those dreams, you inspire others to achieve theirs too? Perhaps your dreams begin to affect other people simply because you achieved them?

What if, by taking control of your life, changing your questions, getting different answers, moving your focus, directing your actions, and ultimately achieving your hopes and dreams, you also begin helping other people do the same? And what if by changing our lives individually and causing the ripple effect of changing the lives of other people, together, we all truly begin to change the world?

What if I'm right?

What if all you have to do is try this for four weeks? Take twenty-eight days to see if it can make a difference in your life?

Go ahead, I dare you!

I double-dog dare you!

Let's Connect

I don't want our time together to end here. I'd love to hear how you're using the tools from the book, what questions are working for you, and if any of them aren't. I'd also love to hear of new questions you've come up with that are particularly helpful.

Either way, I'd love to connect with you and answer any questions you might have.

You can reach me via www.michaeljenet.com.

I look forward to hearing from you and about all that you're accomplishing in your life.

MJ

Journey Institute Press

Journey Institute Press is a non-profit publishing house created by authors to flip the publishing model for new authors. Created with intention and purpose to provide the highest quality publishing resources available to authors whose stories might otherwise not be told.

JI Press focusses on women, BIPOC, and LGBTQ+ authors without regard to the genre of their work.

As a Publishing House, our goal is to create a supportive, nurturing, and encouraging environment that puts the author above the publisher in the publishing model.

Guide Point North Publishing is an Imprint of Journey Institute Press, a division of 50 in 52 Journey, Inc.

9 798989 437917